Guitar Chord Book

Guitar Command

www.GuitarCommand.com

By Laurence Harwood.

Edited by Dan Wright.

Published by Timescale Music

ISBN: 978-0-9556566-4-4

This publication Copyright © 2014 by L. Harwood. All Rights Reserved. This publication may not be copied or distributed in whole or in part without prior written permission from the copyright holder.

Contents

Introduction 4
Guitar Chords 5
How To Read Chord Diagrams 5
Information About Chord Diagrams 6
Tips For Playing Guitar Chords 7
Guitar Fretboard Diagram 8
Basic Guitar Chords 9
   Major Chords 9
   Minor Chords 9
   Dominant 7th Chords 10
Guitar Chords - Quick Reference 10
   Major Chords 11
   Minor (m) Chords 12
   Dominant 7th (7) Chords 13
   Minor 7th (m7) Chords 14
   Major 7th (maj7) Chords 15
   Major 6th (6) Chords 16
   Minor 6th (m6) Chords 17
   Diminished 7th (dim7 or °7) Chords 18
   Dominant 9th (9) Chords 19
   Suspended 4th (sus4) Chords 20
   Suspended 2nd (sus2) Chords 21
   Major Add Nine (add 9) Chords 22
   Minor Add Nine (m add9) Chords 23
   Power Chords (5) 24
Slash Chords 25
Movable Guitar Chords 26
How To Use Movable Chord Shapes 26
   Major Chord Shapes 27
   Minor (m) Chord Shapes 28
   Dominant 7th (7) Chord Shapes 28

Minor 7th (m7) Chord Shapes   29

Power Chord (5) Chord Shapes   29

Suspended 4th (sus4) Chord Shapes   30

Suspended 2nd (sus2) Chord Shapes   30

Dominant 7th Suspended 4th (7sus4) Chord Shapes   30

Major 7th (maj7) Chord Shapes   31

Major 6th (6) Chord Shapes   31

Minor 6th (m6) Chord Shapes   32

Major 6 - 9 (6/9) Chord Shapes   32

Minor 6 - 9 (m6/9) Chord Shapes   32

Minor / Major 7th (m(maj7)) Chord Shapes   33

Major Add Nine (add9) Chord Shapes   33

Minor Add Nine (m add9) Chord Shapes   33

Diminished 7th (dim7 or °7) Chord Shapes   34

Dominant 9th (9) Chord Shapes   34

Dominant 11th (11) Chord Shapes   34

Dominant 13th (13) Chord Shapes   35

Minor 9th (m9) Chord Shapes   35

Minor 11th (m11) Chord Shapes   36

Minor 7th Flat Five (m7♭5) Chord Shapes   36

Three-Note Jazz Chords   37

Dominant 7th Augmented (7aug or 7♯5) Chord Shapes   38

Dominant 7th Sharp Nine (7♯9) Chord Shapes   38

Dominant 7th Sharp Five Flat Nine (7♯5♭9) Chord Shapes   38

Dominant 7th Sharp Five Sharp Nine (7♯5♯9) Chord Shapes   39

Dominant 7th Flat Five (7♭5) Chord Shapes   39

Dominant 7th Flat Nine (7♭9) Chord Shapes   39

Dominant 7th Flat Five Flat Nine (7♭5♭9) Chord Shapes   40

Dominant 9th Sharp Five (9♯5) Chord Shapes   40

Dominant 9th Flat Five (9♭5) Chord Shapes   40

Dominant 13th Flat Five (13♭5) Chord Shapes   41

Dominant 13th Flat Nine (13♭9) Chord Shapes   41

Dominant 13th Sharp Eleven (13♯11) Chord Shapes   41

Introduction

The *Guitar Chord Book* contains a large number of guitar chords presented in diagram form. You can work through the book from beginning to end to improve your chord knowledge, or use it to find specific chords whenever you need them.

This book is suitable for electric and acoustic guitarists of all styles and abilities. Use it to learn: basic chords for playing and writing songs; barre chords for rock, pop and metal; complex jazz chords for creative comping; and chords suitable for use in many other musical situations.

The chords in this book are presented in diagram form: you do not have to read music to use the book.

We hope that you enjoy using this book and that your playing benefits from the information it contains.

Guitar Command

Guitar Command is a website and specialist guitar publisher.

Visit **www.GuitarCommand.com** for guitar news, information and free lessons. Improve your lead guitar playing with **Guitar Command Backing Track** albums, available to download from online stores.

Also Available

Guitar Scale Book

A comprehensive resource for improvising guitarists. Contains diagrams and tab for basic and exotic scales, including pentatonic, major, minor, blues, modes, Japanese and jazz scales.
ISBN: 978-0-9556566-5-1

Guitar Chords, Scales & Arpeggios: The Complete Guitar Reference Book

A complete reference book for all guitarists. Contains all of the information from the *Guitar Chord Book* and the *Guitar Scale Book* in one volume.
ISBN: 978-0-9556566-6-8

Guitar Chords

This book contains a comprehensive collection of guitar chords for use in all styles of music. The book is in three sections:

1. Basic Guitar Chords

This section contains a selection of open-position chords. These are relatively easy to play and should be among the first chords a beginner guitarist learns.

2. Guitar Chords Quick Reference

Use this section to find the chord you need quickly and easily. Diagrams of all of the common types of chord are included with every root note. Alternative ways of playing each type of chord are provided in the Movable Chord Shapes section.

3. Movable Chord Shapes

This section contains movable shapes for a large number of chords. Movable chord shapes can be moved up and down the fretboard in order to play the same type of chord (e.g. major, minor, etc.) with a different root note.

How To Read Chord Diagrams

Guitar chord diagrams represent the guitar fretboard. They show where the fretting fingers should be placed in order to play a chord.

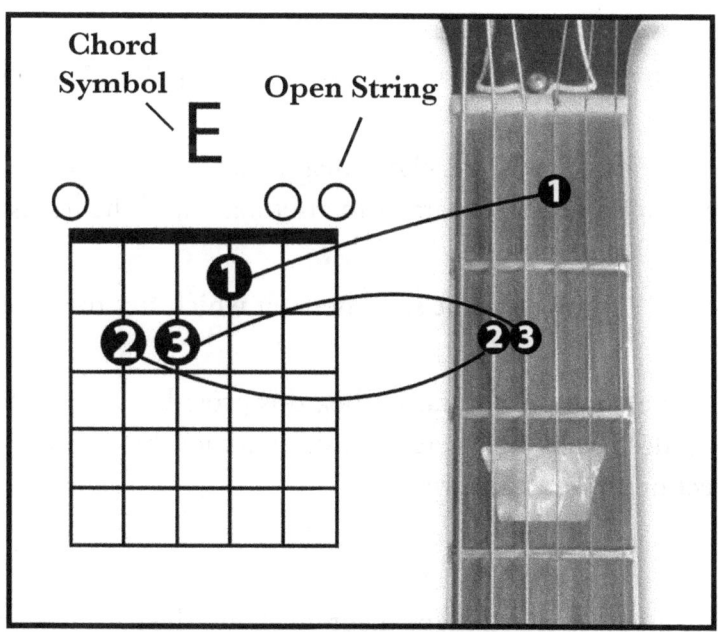

How A Chord Diagram Relates To The Guitar Neck

Standard Fretting Finger Numbering

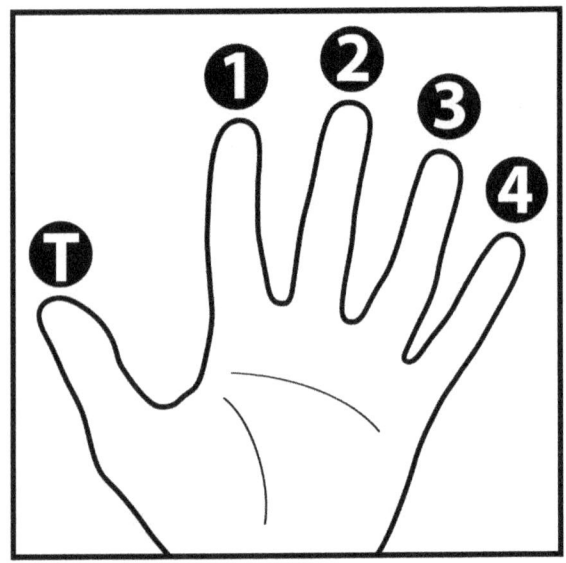

1: Index Finger
2: Middle Finger
3: Ring Finger
4: Little Finger
T: Thumb

The chord fingerings in this book are provided as suggestions only; feel free to experiment with your own.

Information About Chord Diagrams

The vertical lines in a chord diagram represent the guitar strings, with the bottom E string on the left. The horizontal lines are the frets.

The black circles show where the fingers should be placed; the numbers inside these circles show which fingers should be used.

A circle or 'O' above a string shows that the string is played as part of the chord but is not fingered, i.e. it is left 'open'.

An 'X' above a string means that the string should not be played. Avoid hitting it with your plectrum or fingers when you strum the chord, or stop it from ringing with another fretting finger.

A thicker horizontal line on the top of some chord diagrams represents the 'nut' of the guitar. The nut is the grooved ridge that separates the fretboard and the headstock. Position your fingers in relation to the nut.

For diagrams without a nut, a number to the side shows at which fret the chord should be played.

A diagram showing all of the notes on a guitar fretboard is provided on page 8. Refer to this diagram when you need to know where to position a movable chord shape. See the 'Movable Chords' section for more information.

Root Notes

An 'R' next to a note in a movable chord shape diagram shows the **root note** of the chord. The root note of a chord is the note that gives the chord its name, i.e. the 'C' of C major, or the 'G' of G minor 9th.

Tips For Playing Guitar Chords

- *Experiment with where you put your fingers in the frets. Positioning fingers closer to the fretwire (towards the right of the fret on a standard, right-handed guitar) can minimise fretbuzz and make chords easier to play.*

- *When you are learning a chord, try playing the notes one at a time rather than all at once. This will let you know if every note in the chord is sounding correctly. If any notes sound dull or are not sounding at all, shuffle your fingers around until all of the notes ring out clearly.*

- *Remember, if you are having problems getting all of the notes to sound, it is usually a case of moving your fingers around to find a more efficient position rather than simply pressing down harder.*

- *Learning just one movable chord shape means that you can play that chord with any root note. Therefore, if you learn a movable major chord shape, you can play any major chord!*

- *However, to avoid either playing chords too high up the fretboard or having to jump around the fretboard too much, it is always useful to know more than one way of playing each type of chord.*

Which Chord Shape To Use?

Most types of chord can be played in several different ways. For example, a C major chord can be played in open position or further up the fretboard as a movable chord.

Printed music often specifies only the *type* of chord to be played rather than the actual chord shape to be used. It is left up to the guitarist to decide how to play the chord.

Open position chords can sound brighter and are often easier to play than barre chords, particularly on acoustic guitars. However, they are not as easy to dampen for complex rhythmic patterns and their sound can be overbearing in some situations.

Barre chords and other movable shapes are more versatile but can sound less 'full' and can be harder to move to and from smoothly.

There are no hard and fast rules for selecting which chord shape to use. Your choice will depend on the style of music, the strumming pattern you are using, the tempo of the song and the sound of the chord. The best advice as always is to let your ears be the judge.

Guitar Fretboard Diagram

Use the guitar fretboard diagram below to position movable chord shapes. Standard string numbering is used, from 6 (the low E string) to 1 (the high E string).

The shaded areas on the diagram represent the frets which, on most guitars, contain dots or other inlaid markers.

String

	6	5	4	3	2	1
Open	E	A	D	G	B	E
1	F	A#/Bb	D#/Eb	G#/Ab	C	F
2	F#/Gb	B	E	A	C#/Db	F#/Gb
3	G	C	F	A#/Bb	D	G
4	G#/Ab	C#/Db	F#/Gb	B	D#/Eb	G#/Ab
5	A	D	G	C	E	A
6	A#/Bb	D#/Eb	G#/Ab	C#/Db	F	A#/Bb
7	B	E	A	D	F#/Gb	B
8	C	F	A#/Bb	D#/Eb	G	C
9	C#/Db	F#/Gb	B	E	G#/Ab	C#/Db
10	D	G	C	F	A	D
11	D#/Eb	G#/Ab	C#/Db	F#/Gb	A#/Bb	D#/Eb
12	E	A	D	G	B	E

Fret Number

(At the 12th fret, notes are repeated an octave higher.)

Basic Guitar Chords

These chords are among the first a guitarist should learn. However, they're not just for beginners – most guitarists will continue to use these chords throughout their careers.

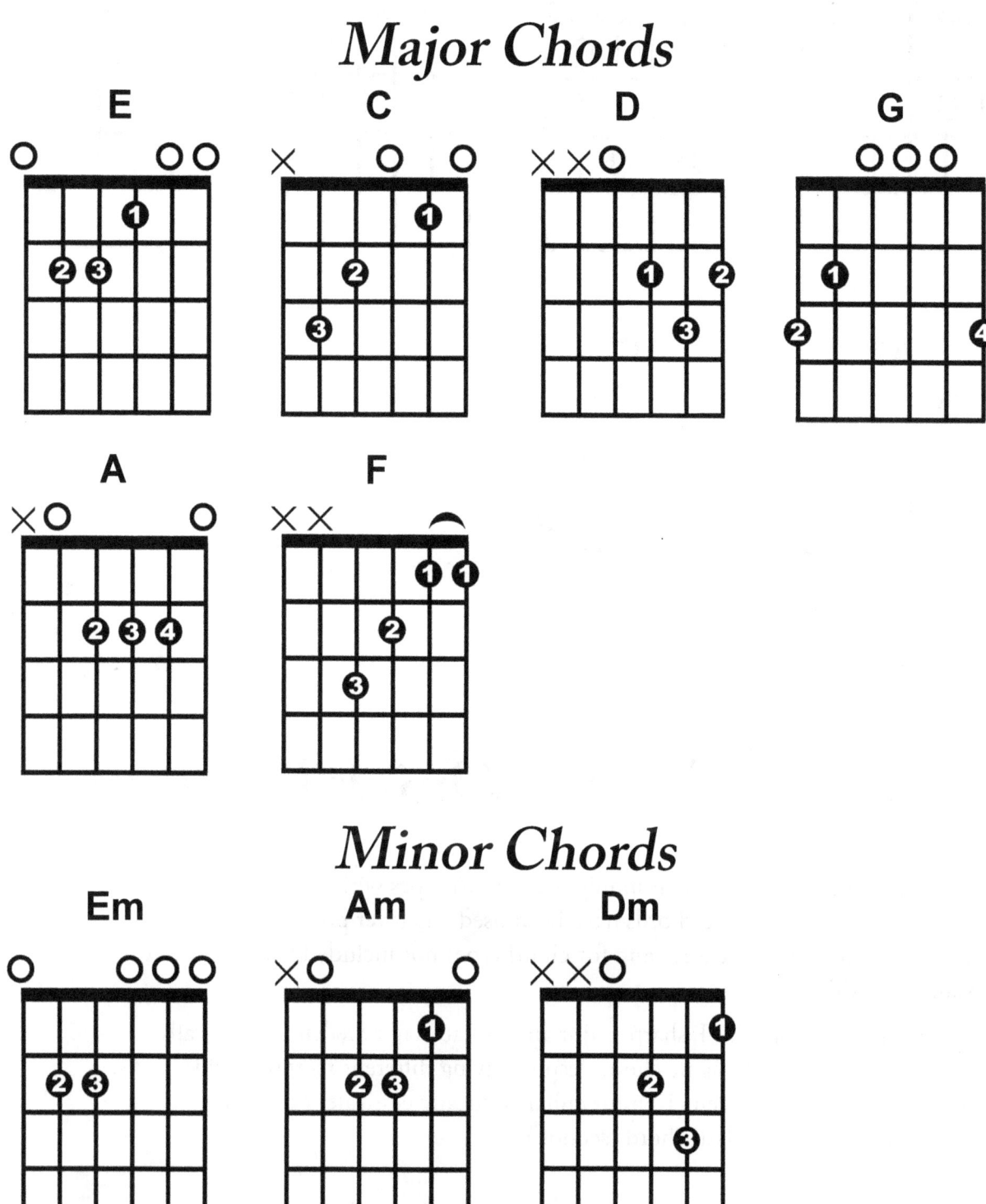

Dominant 7th Chords

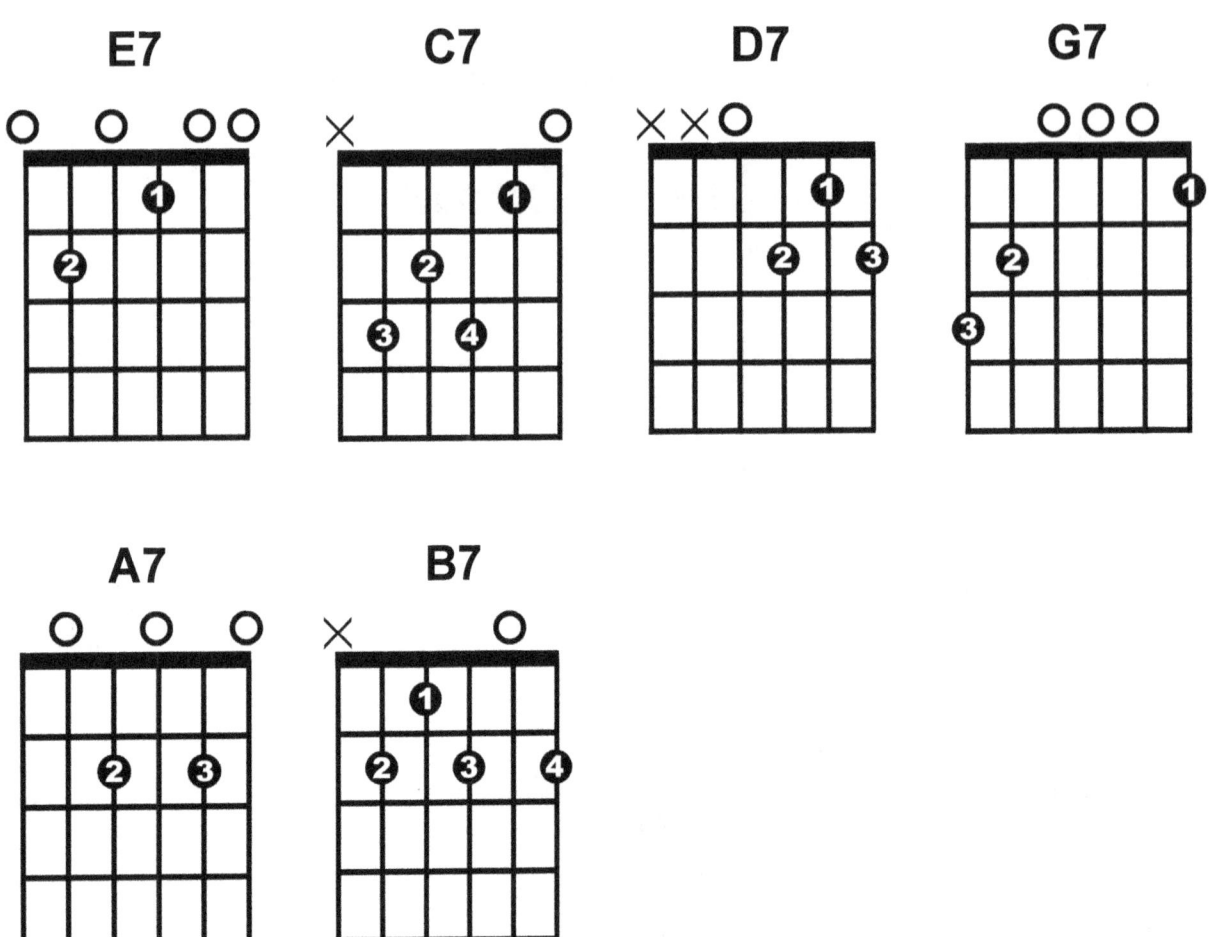

Guitar Chords - Quick Reference

This section contains all of the commonly used chord types with every root note. Open-position versions of the chords have been used wherever possible. For alternative versions of each chord, and for chord types not included here, refer to the 'Movable Chords' section.

Note: pairs of chords such as F sharp major and G flat major are 'enharmonically equivalent', i.e. they are the same chord despite having different names. In this chapter, both names have been given for enharmonically equivalent chords. They are not 'slash chords' (see the slash chords section).

Major Chords

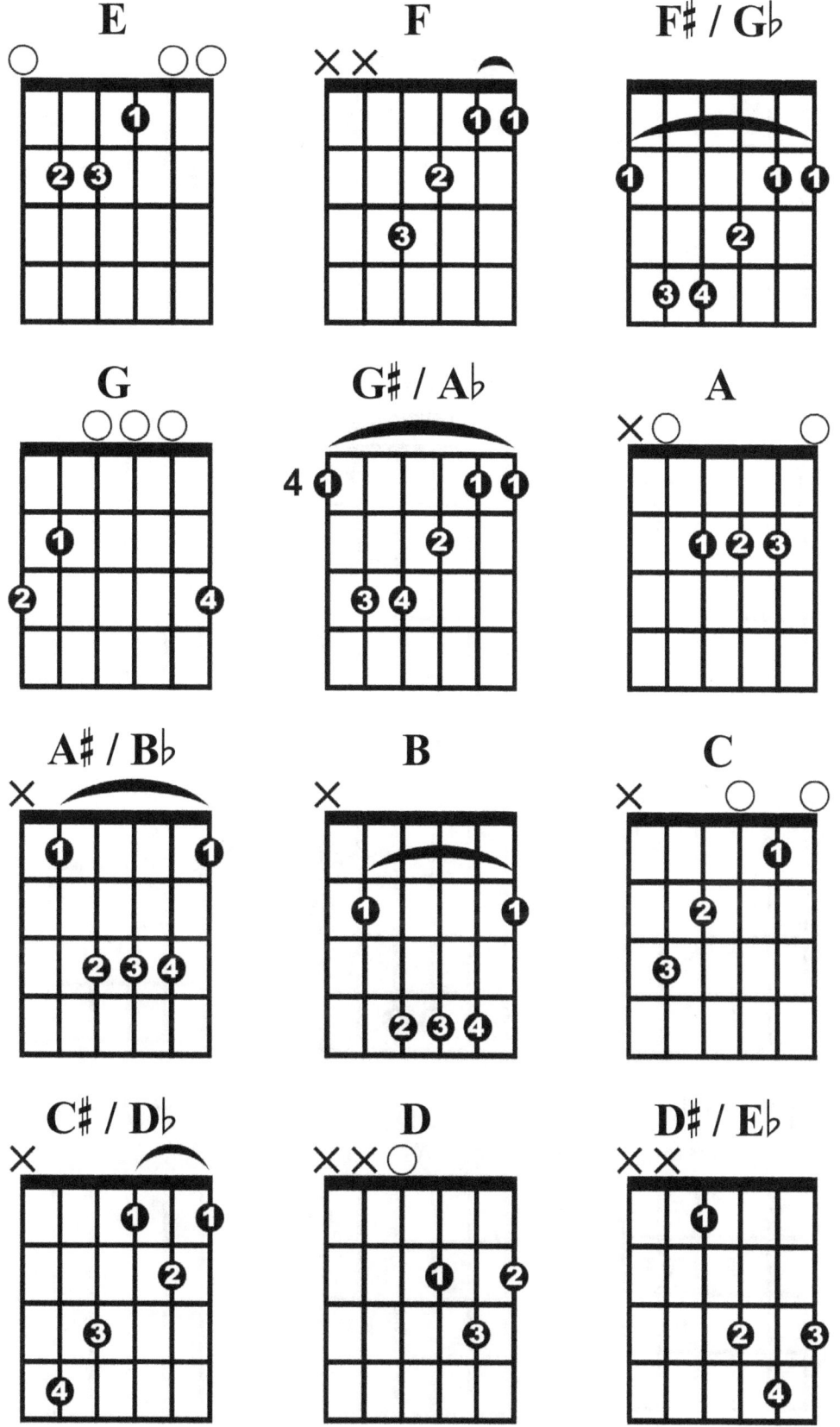

Minor (m) Chords

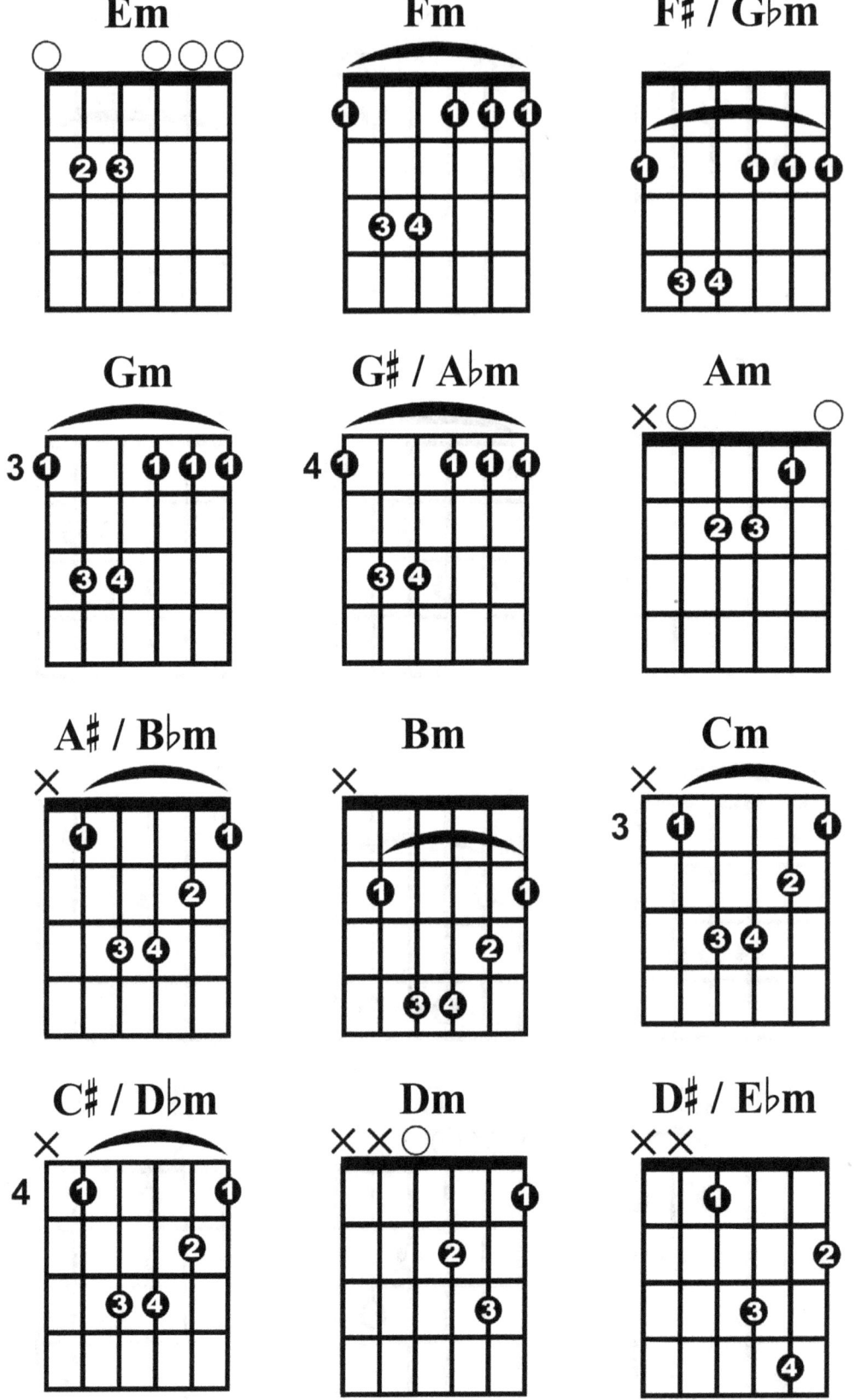

Dominant 7th (7) Chords

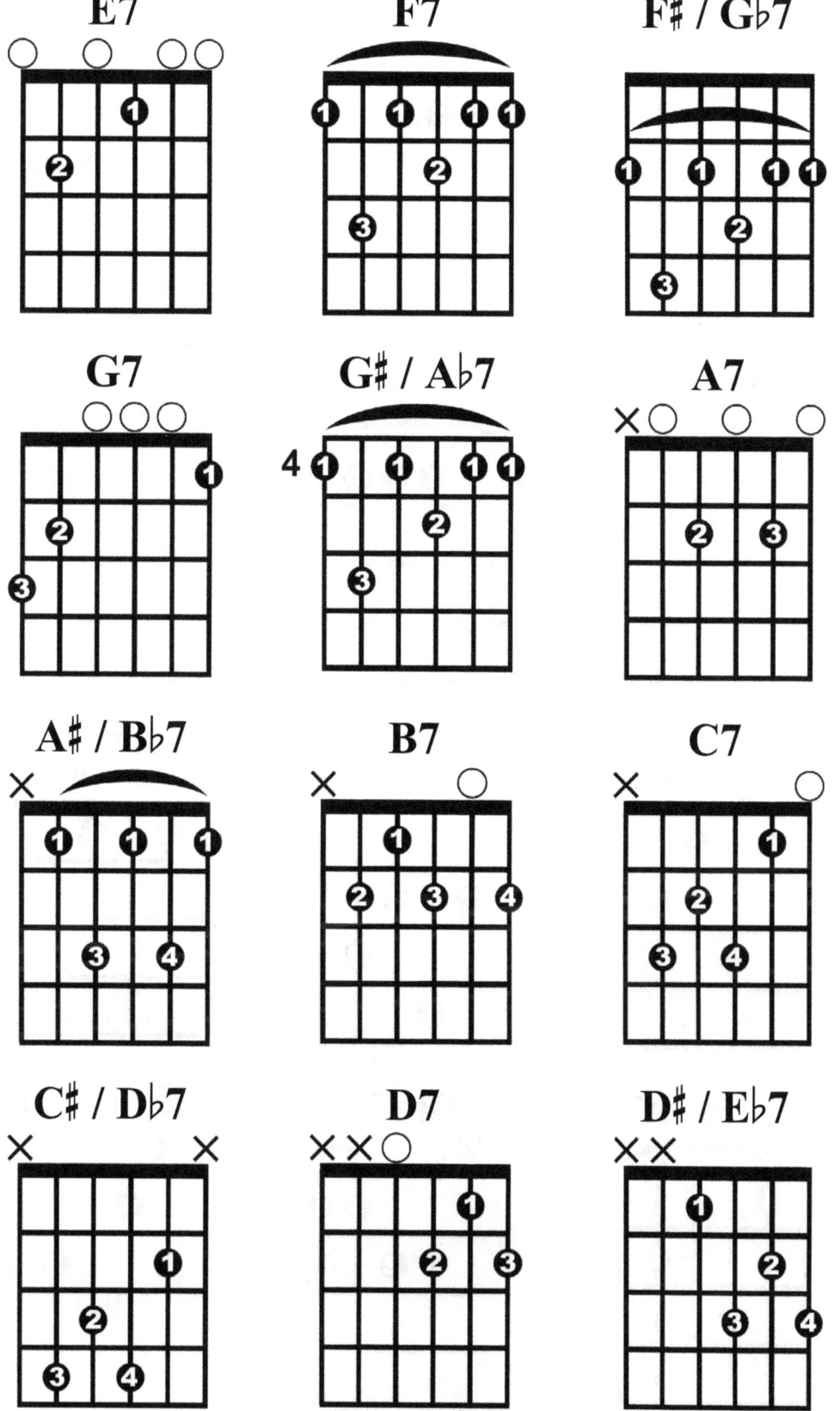

Minor 7th (m7) Chords

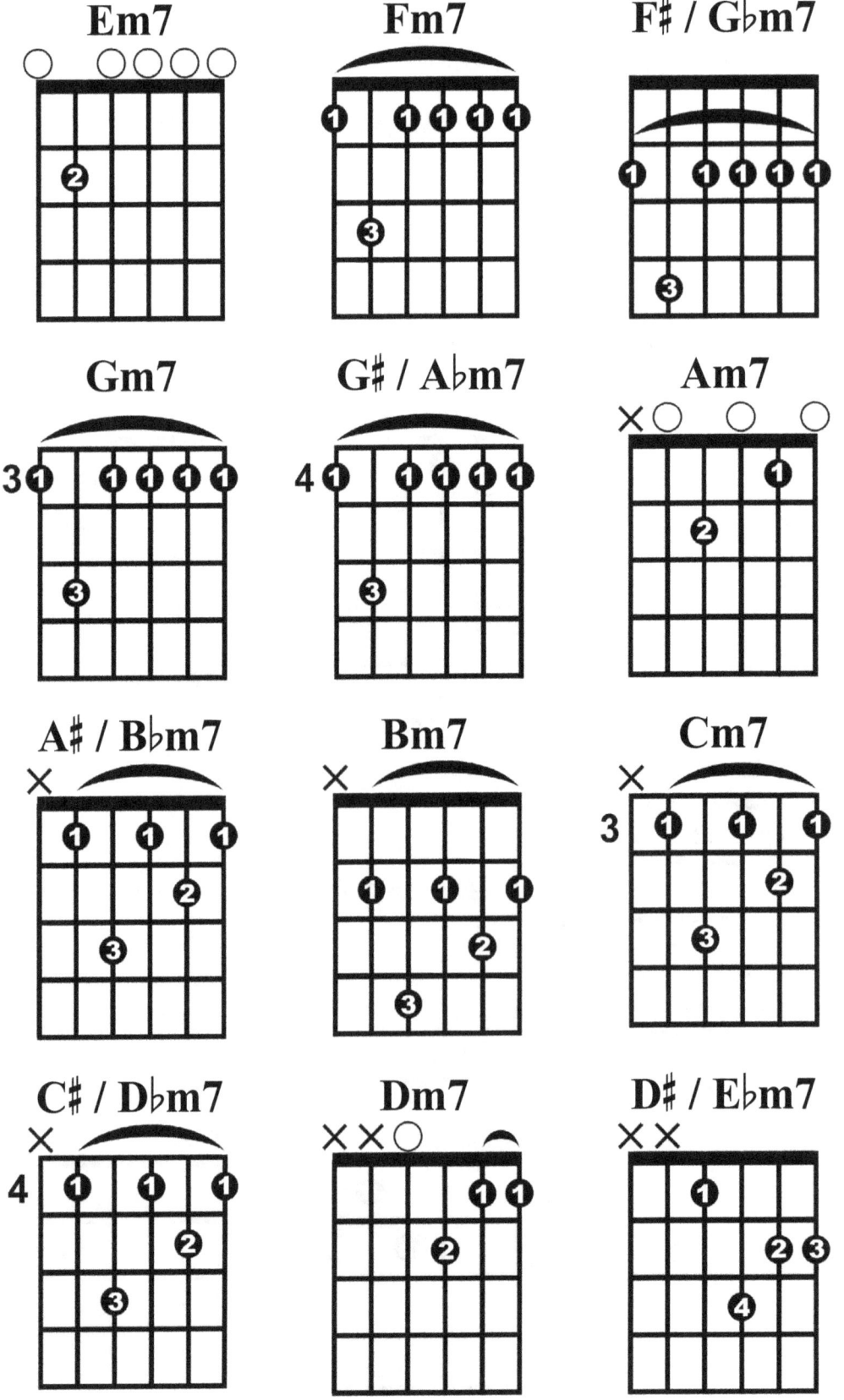

Major 7th (maj7) Chords

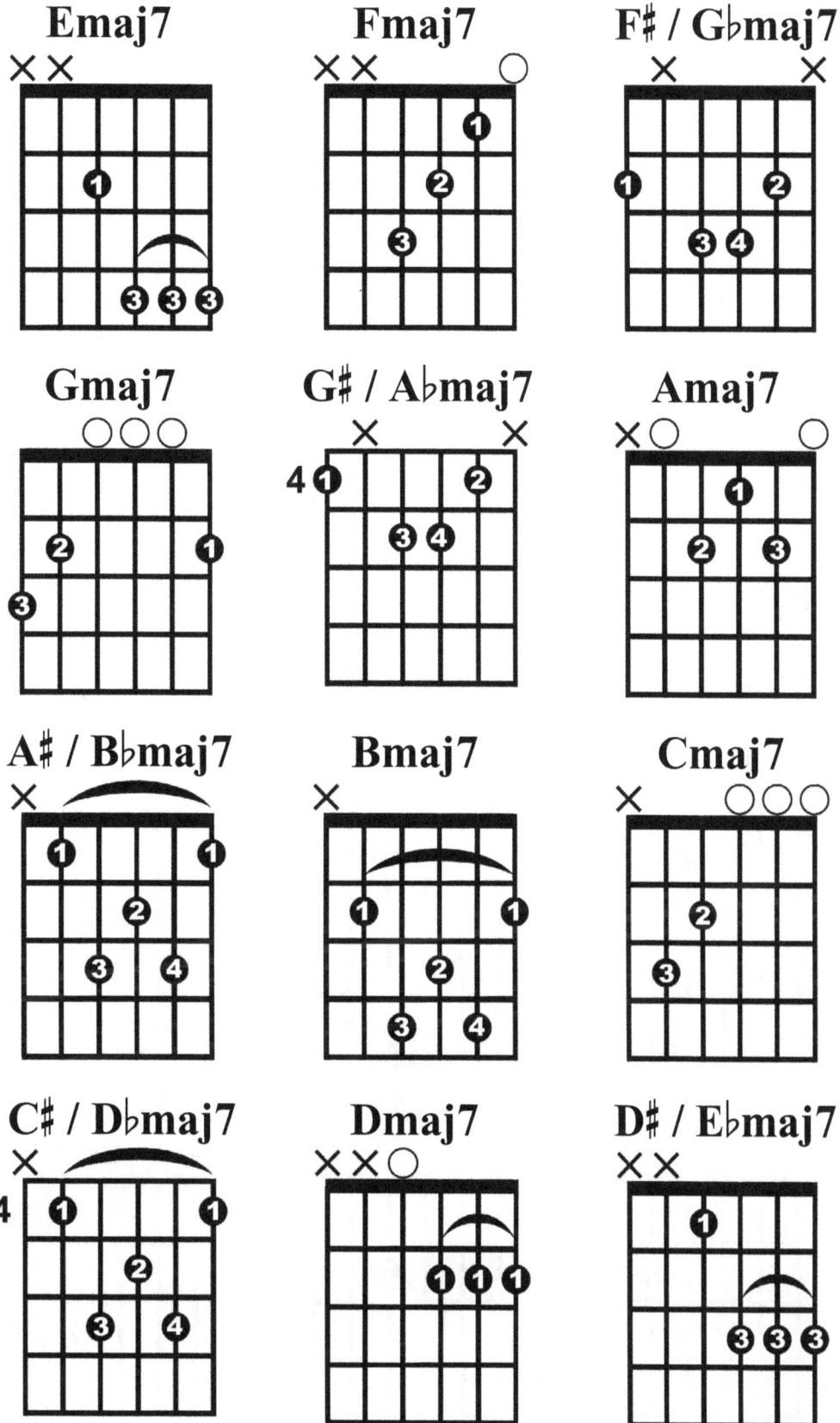

Major 6th (6) Chords

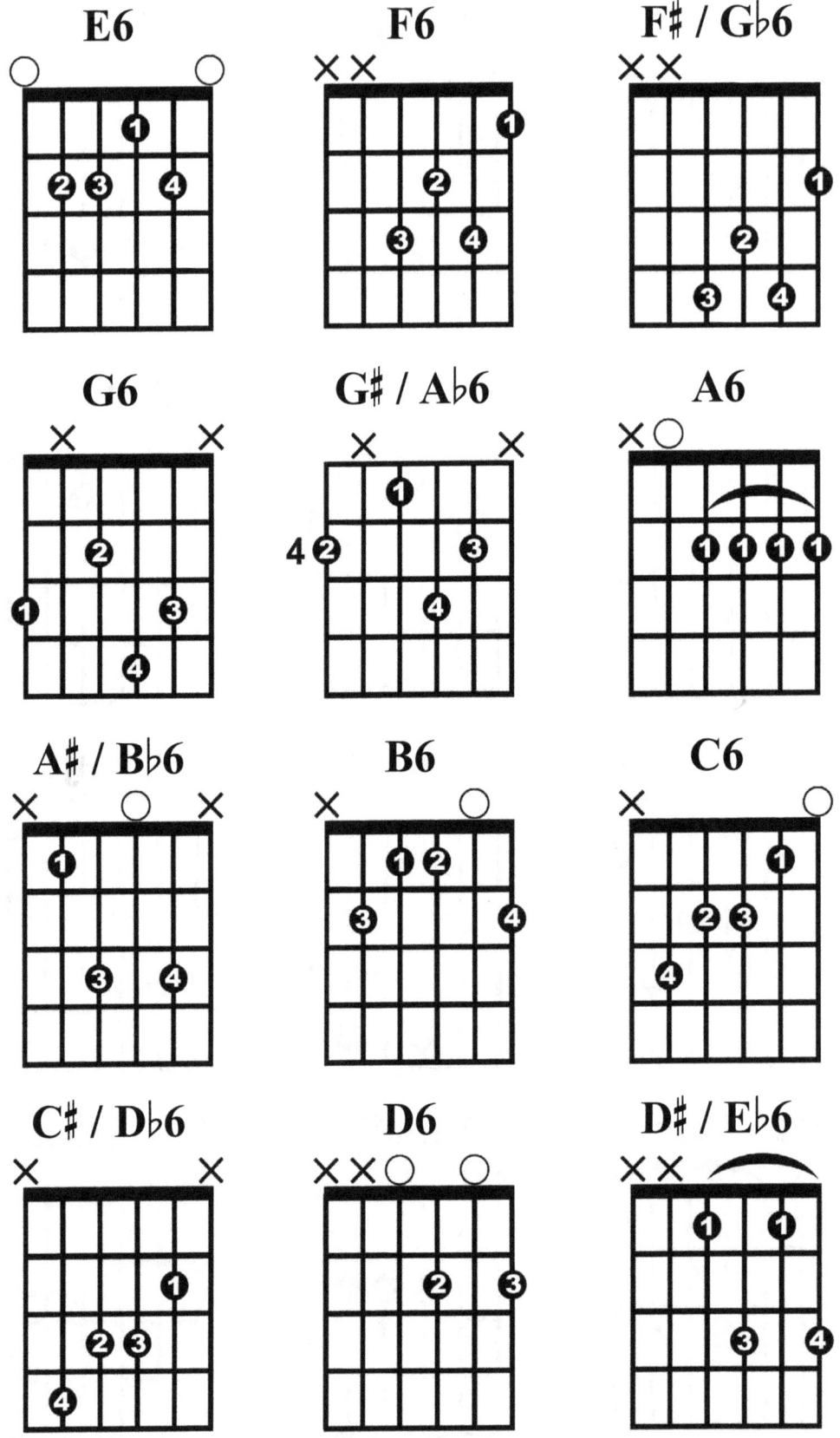

Minor 6th (m6) Chords

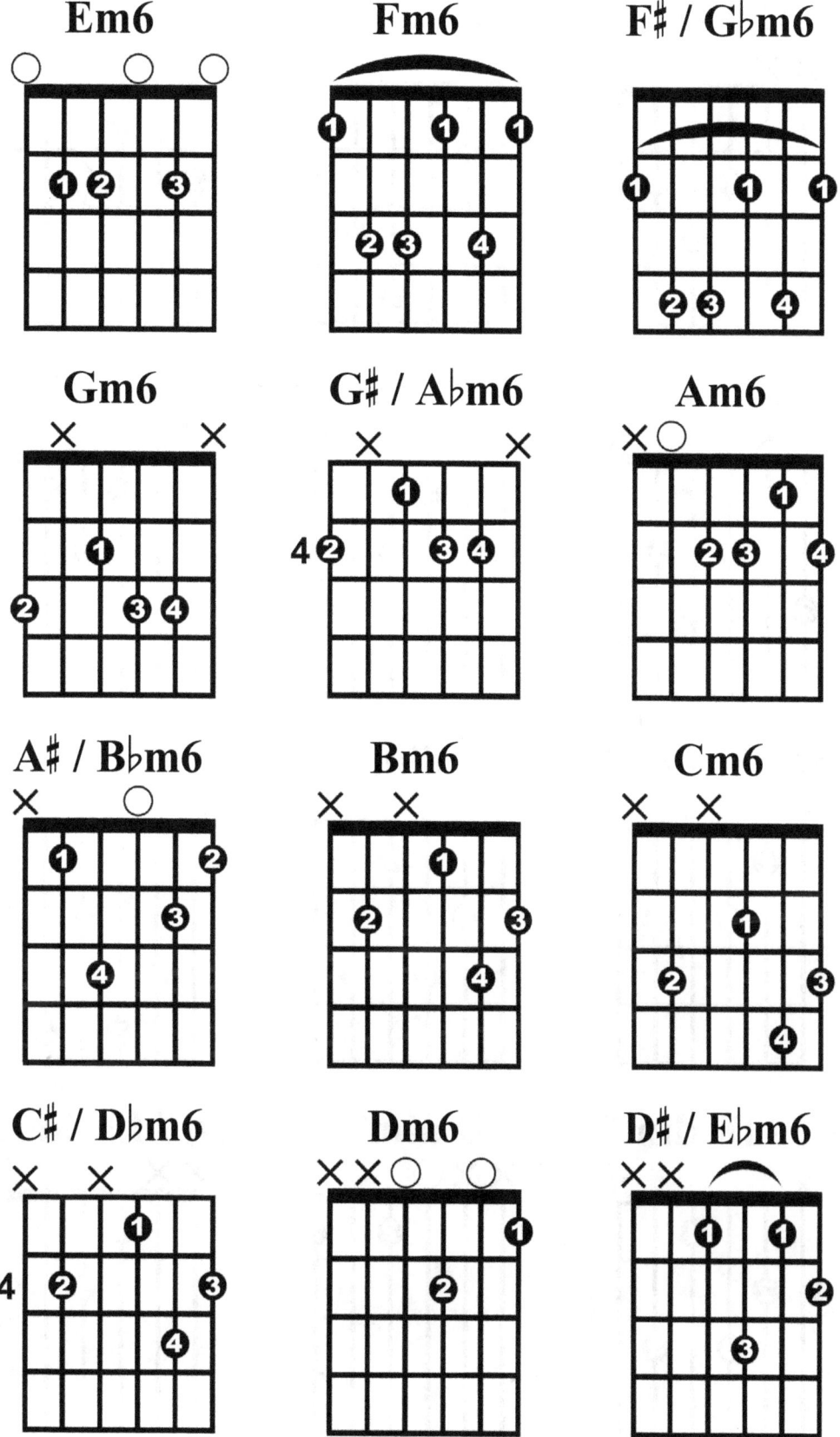

Diminished 7th (dim7 or °7) Chords

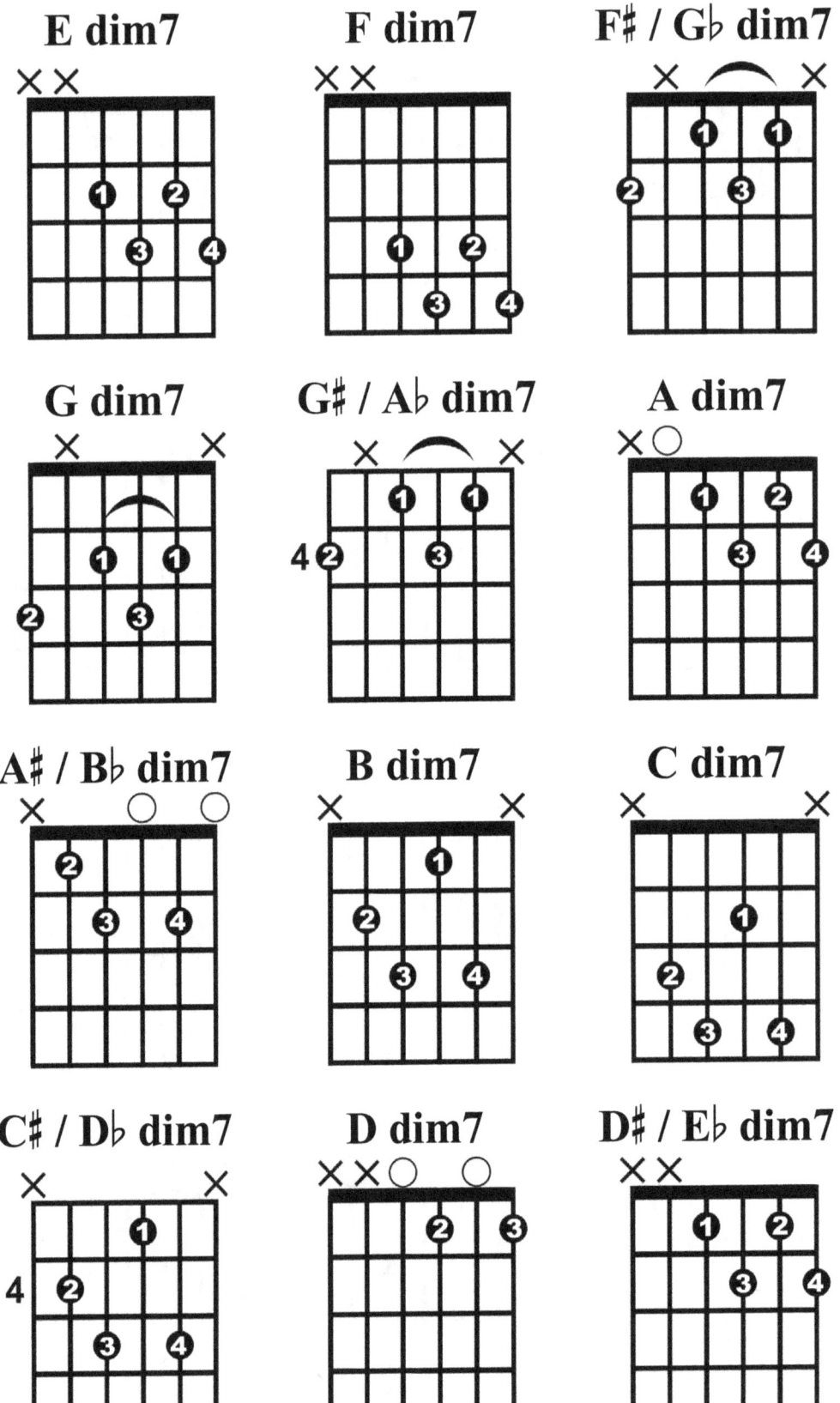

Dominant 9th (9) Chords

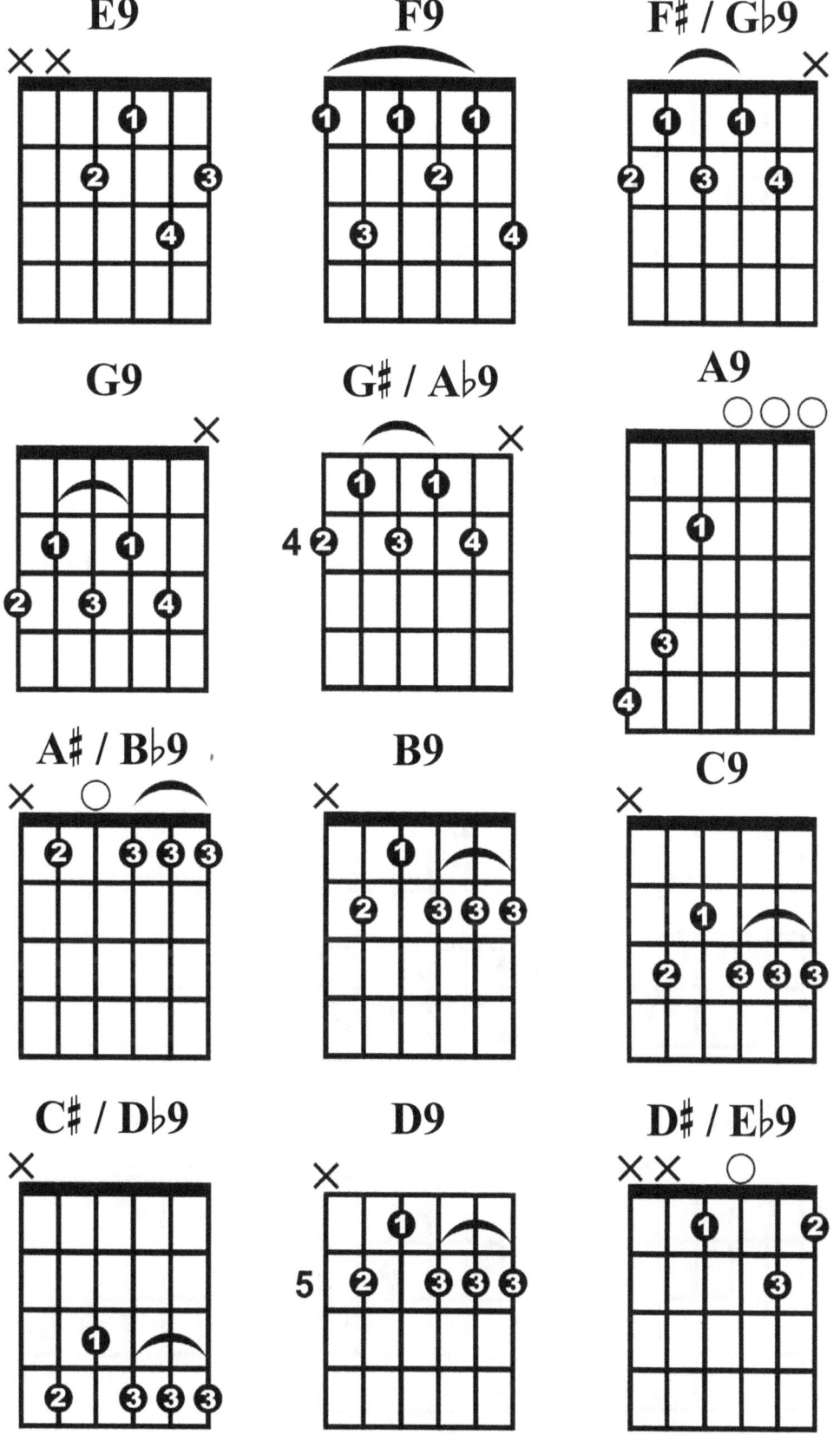

Suspended 4th (sus4) Chords

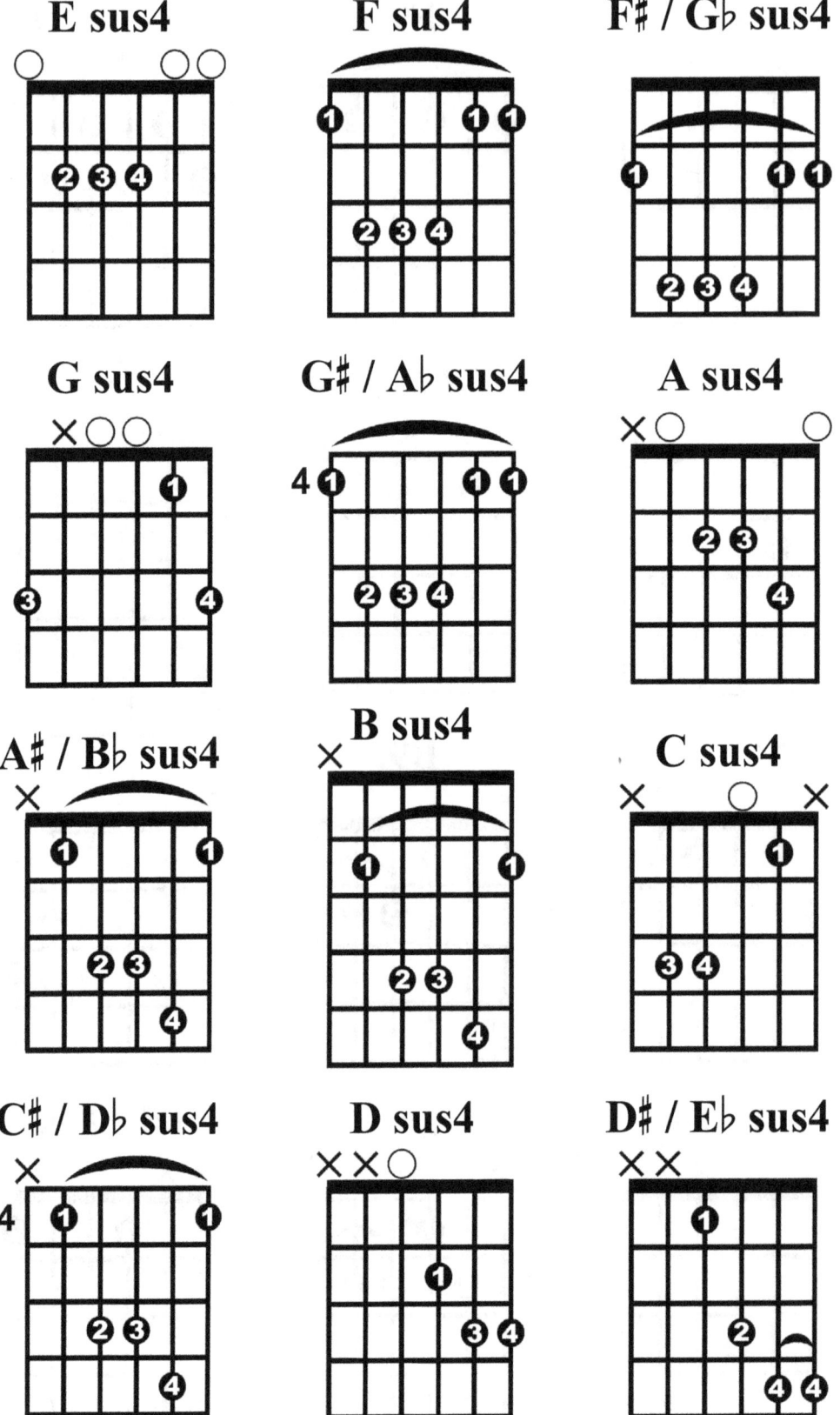

Suspended 2nd (sus2) Chords

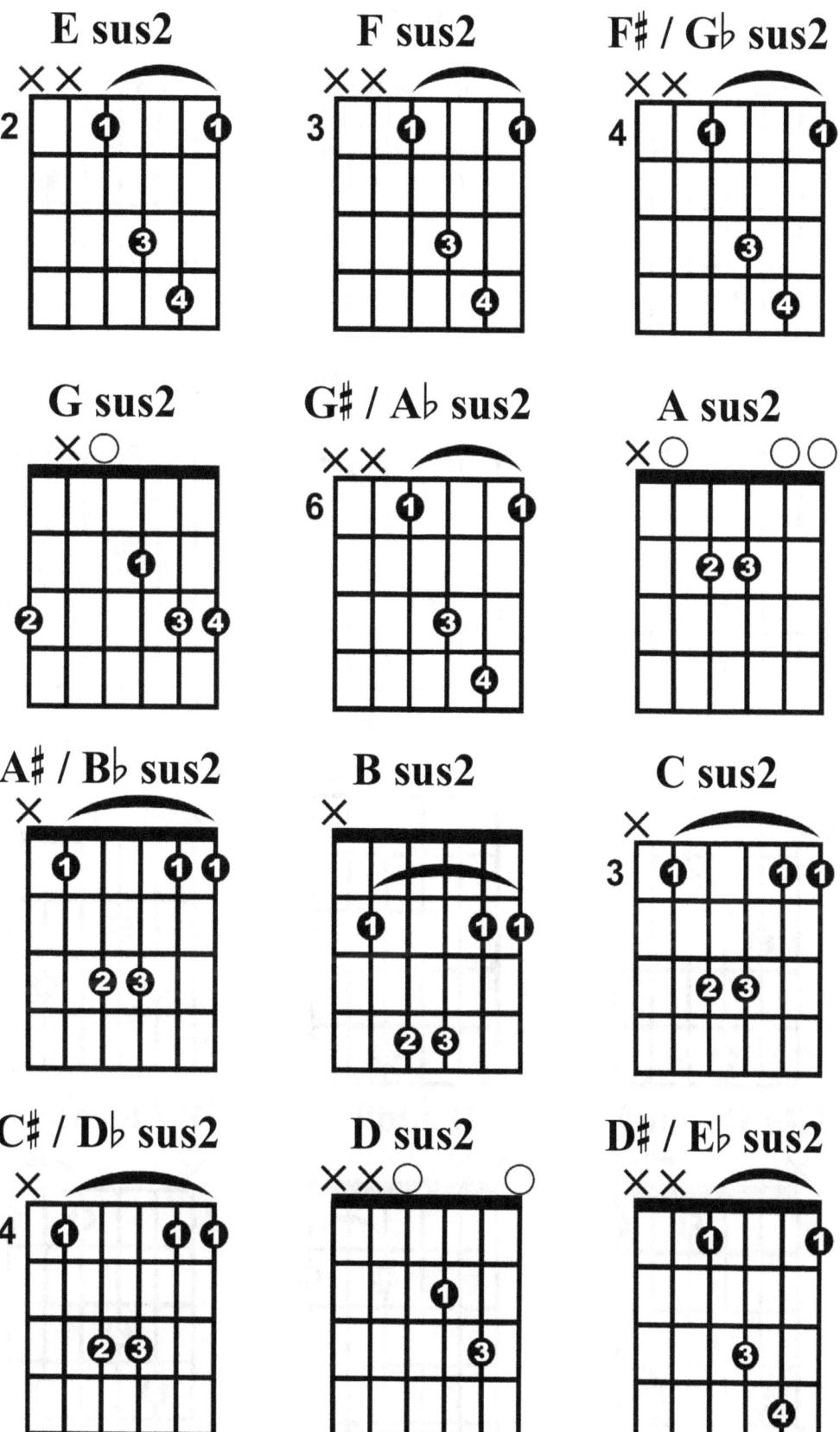

Major Add Nine (add 9) Chords

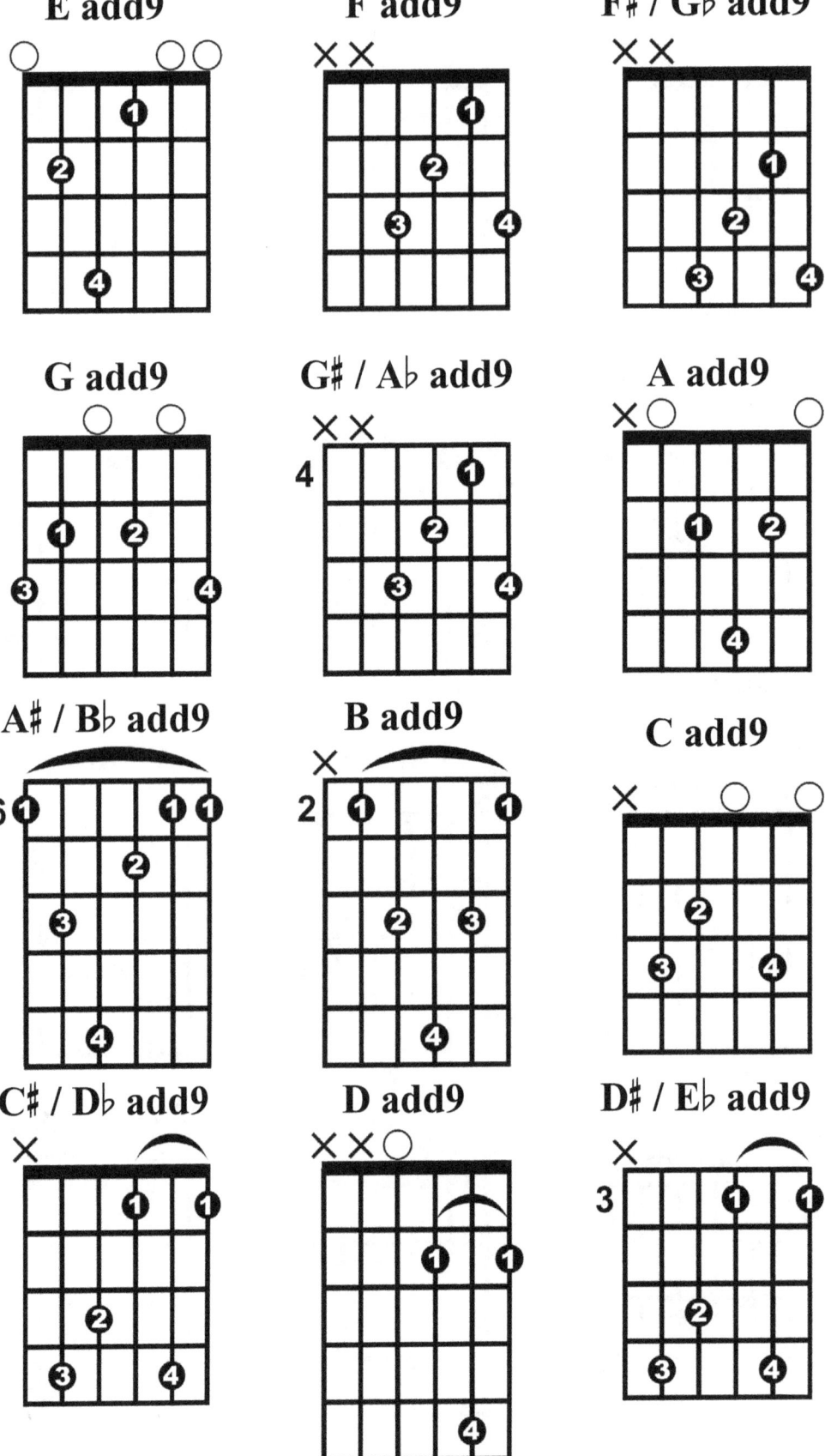

Minor Add Nine (m add9) Chords

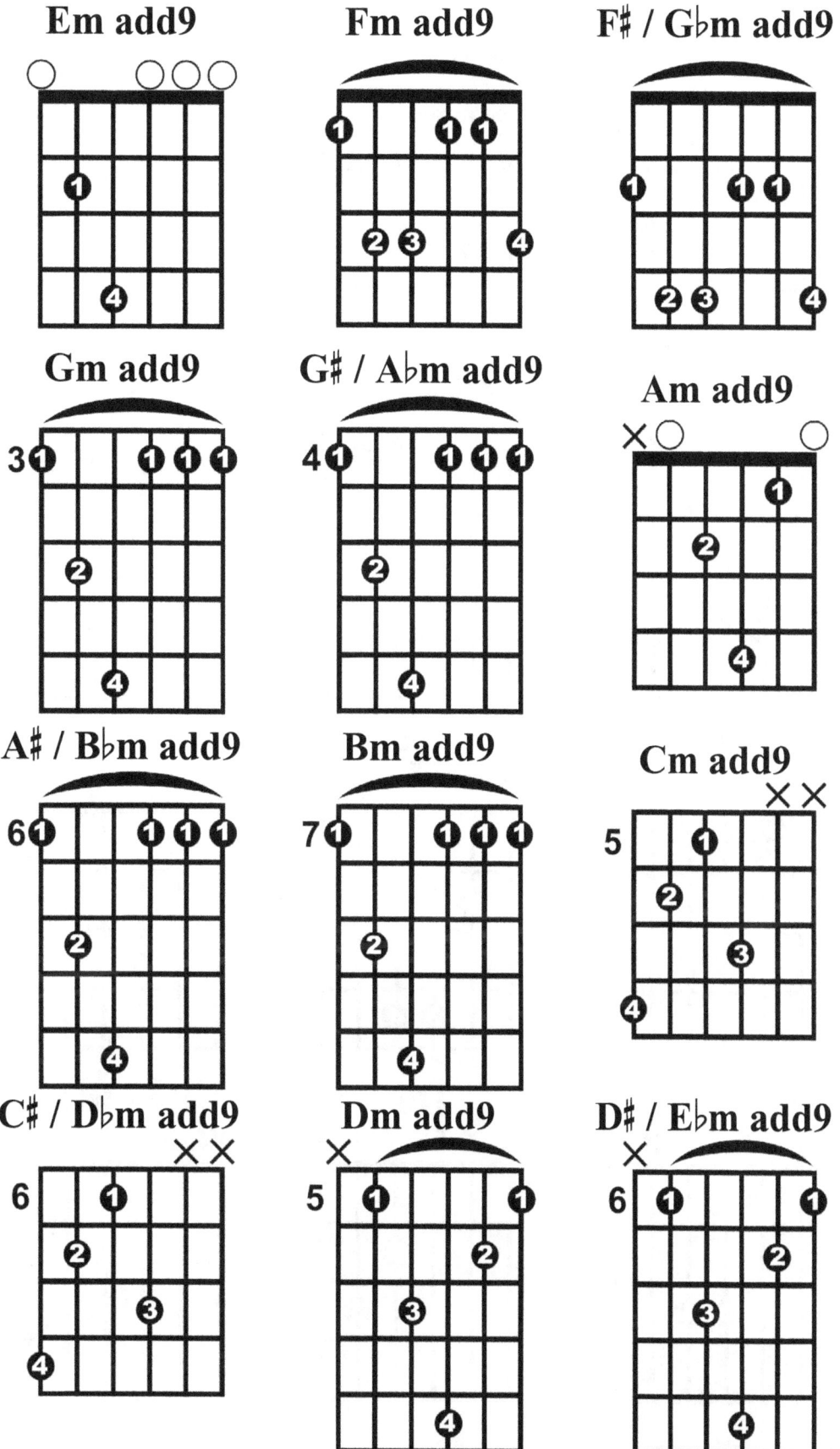

Power Chords (5)

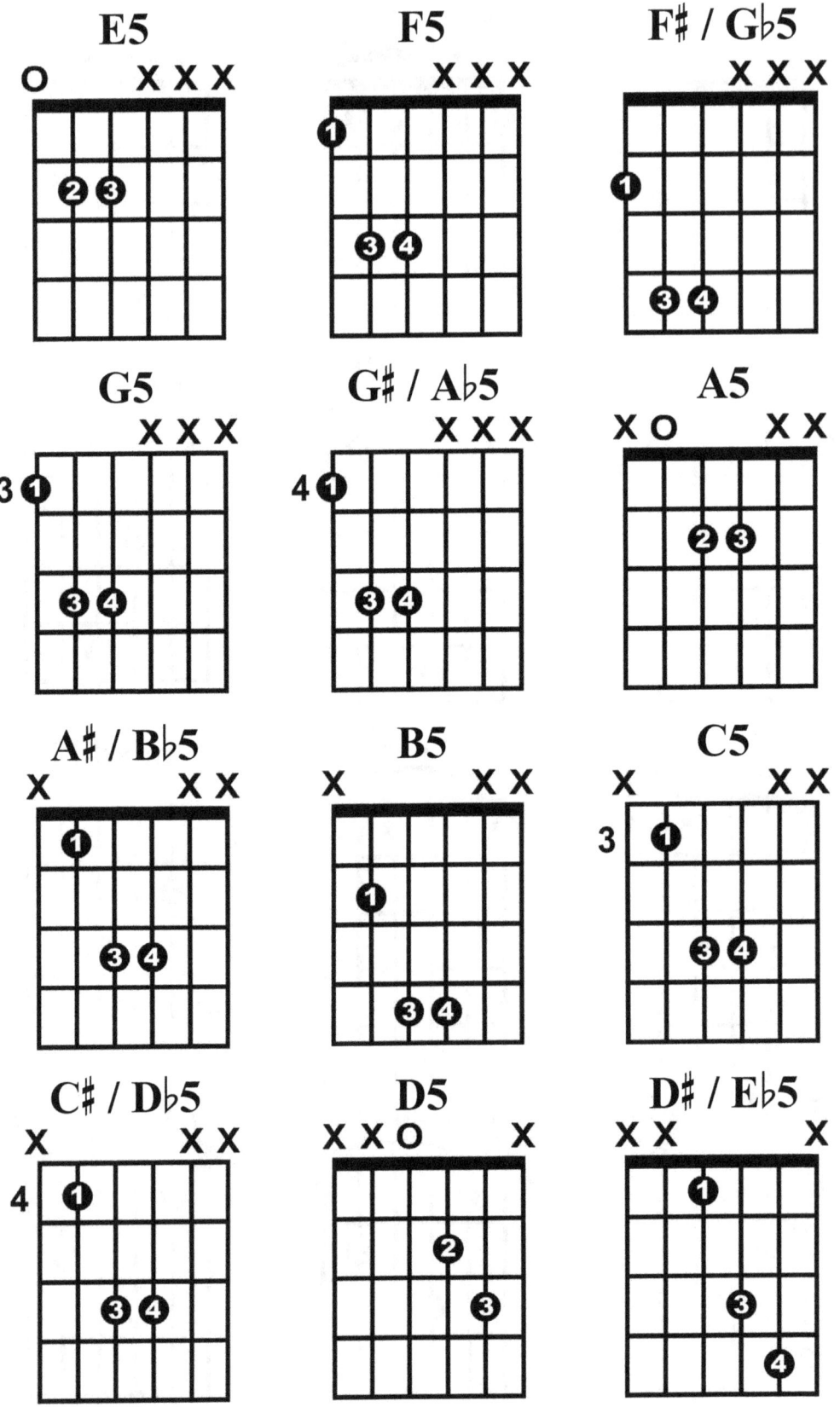

Slash Chords

Slash chord symbols specify both the chord itself, and a bass note that should be added to the chord. For example, a D/F♯ slash chord is a D major chord with an F sharp as the lowest note. An Am/E chord is an A minor chord with an E in the bass.

Slash chords can be any chord with any bass note. Consult the fretboard diagram on page 8 if you are unsure where to play the slash note. Some common slash chords are shown below.

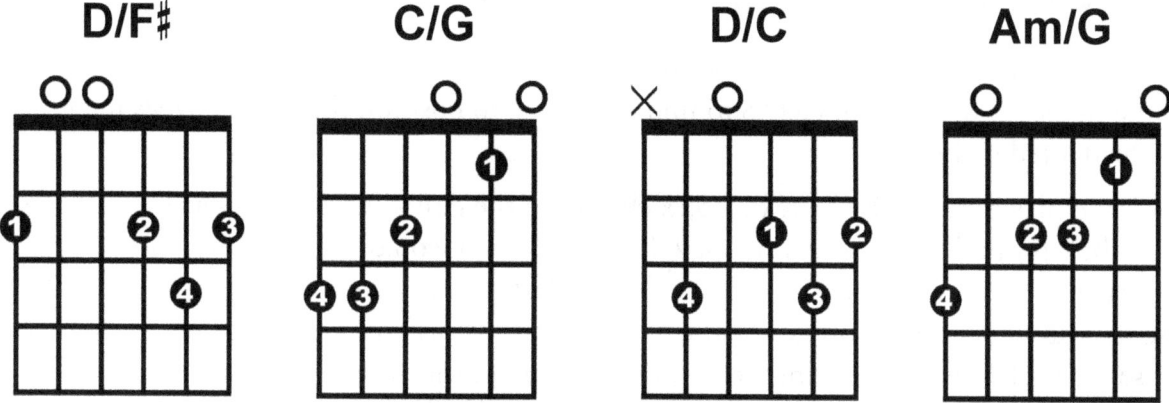

Movable Guitar Chords

The chords in this section of the book are all movable chord shapes. Movable chord shapes can be moved up and down the fretboard to make different chords. For example, the same movable major chord shape that produces a G major chord at the third fret will produce an A major chord if it is played two frets higher, at the fifth fret.

Many movable chord shapes require the use of a 'barre'. This is when a finger (usually the index finger) is placed across the fretboard and used to play more than one note at a time. Barres are represented by curved lines on chord diagrams.

Notes On Movable Chord Shapes

In all of the following diagrams, the root note of a chord shape is shown with an 'R'. Use the fretboard diagram on page 8 to find out where to position the chord shapes to play the desired chord.

In order to play some of the more complex chords on the guitar, notes occasionally have to be left out. This is because to play the whole chord would require either more guitar strings or more fingers than we actually have! The notes that are omitted are those that do not affect the overall nature of the chord. Occasionally, the root notes themselves are left out. Where this occurs, the position of the omitted root note is marked with an R in brackets: **(R)**. This allows the chord to be correctly positioned on the fretboard.

How To Use Movable Chord Shapes

To play a G major chord using the movable shape shown below, position the root note marked on the chord diagram over the G note on the 6th string.

Use the fretboard diagram on page 8 to locate the desired note if necessary.

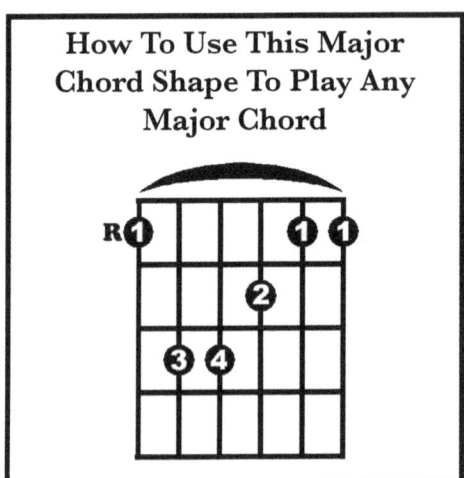

How To Use This Major Chord Shape To Play Any Major Chord

The root note of the chord shape is on the 6th string. There is a G at the third fret of the sixth string, therefore the shape should be played at the third fret for a G major chord.

The other fingers are positioned relative to the root note as shown in the diagram.

To play an A major chord using the same chord shape, the process is repeated, but this time the root note of the chord is positioned over an A note on the 6th string.

The A is two frets higher up the 6th string, at the fifth fret. Therefore, the whole chord shape is moved two frets higher to play an A major chord.

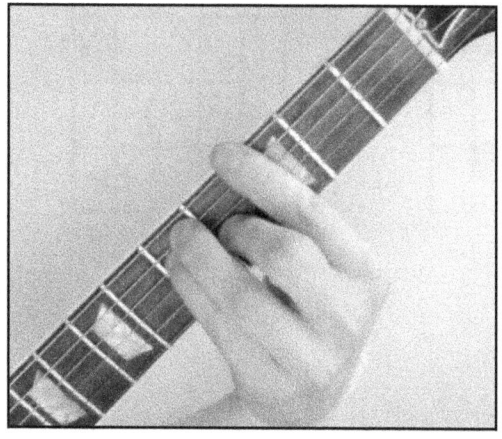

At the third fret, the major chord shape produces a G major chord.

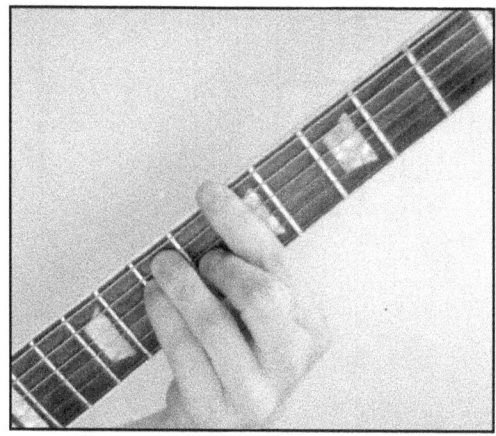

The same major chord shape, when played at the fifth fret, produces an A major chord.

The same shape can be used to play any major chord. For example, moving the same shape another two frets up the fretboard would produce a B major chord.

Major Chord Shapes

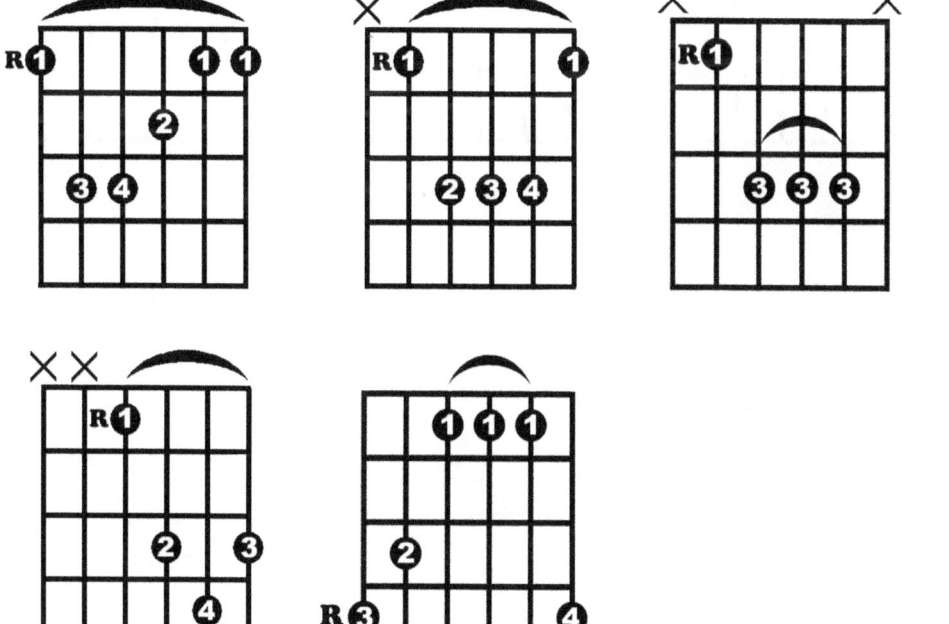

Minor (m) Chord Shapes

 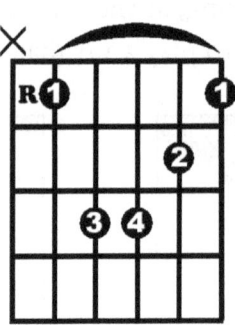 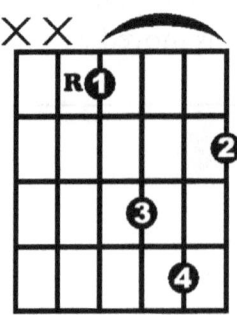

Dominant 7th (7) Chord Shapes

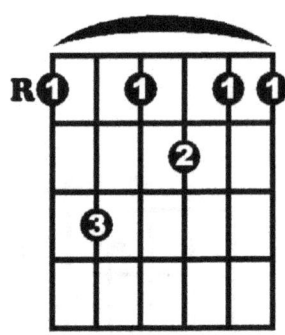 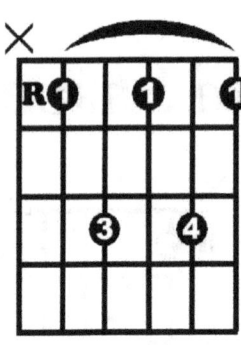 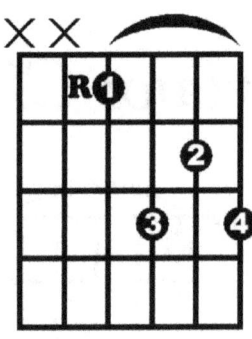 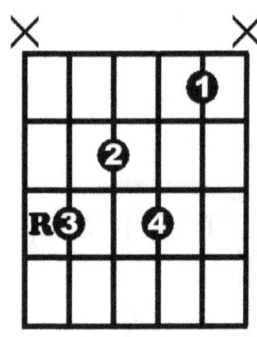

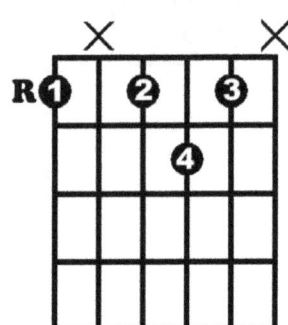

Minor 7th (m7) Chord Shapes

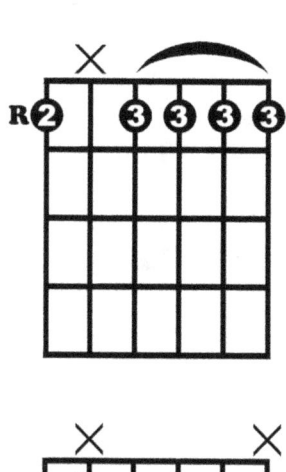 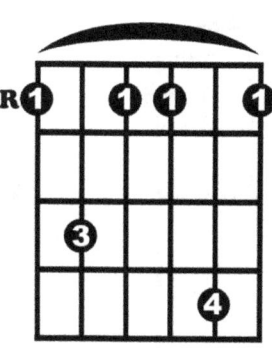 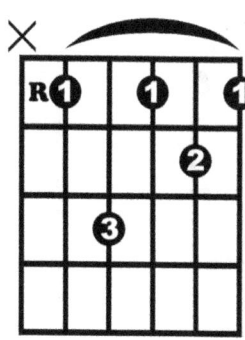 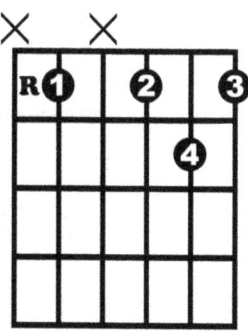

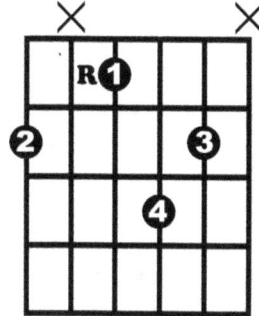 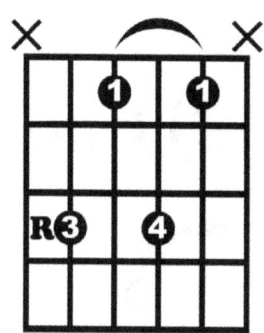

Minor 7th chords can also be written with a dash '-' instead of an 'm', e.g. D-7

Power Chord (5) Chord Shapes

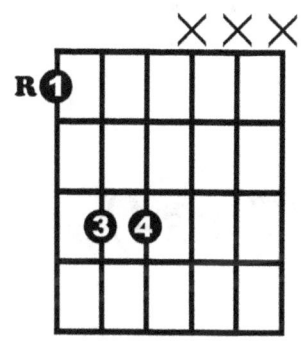 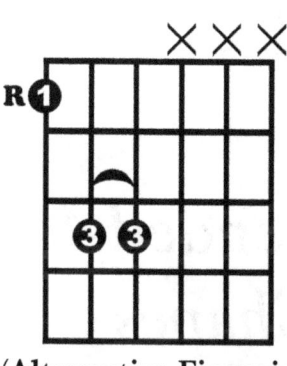 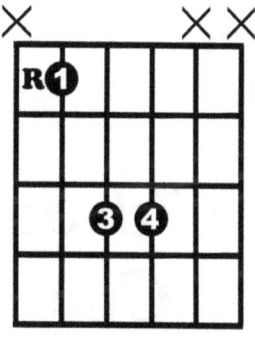 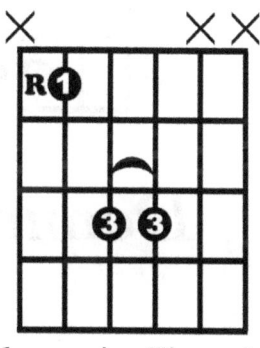

(Alternative Fingering)   (Alternative Fingering)

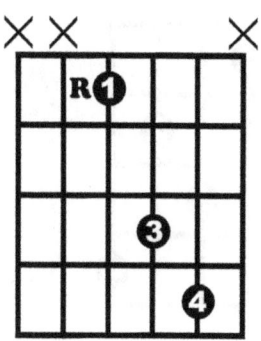

As their name suggests, power chords have a powerful sound, ideal for use in rock and metal. Power chords are also known as fifth chords, as they contain only the root and fifth notes.

Suspended 4th (sus4) Chord Shapes

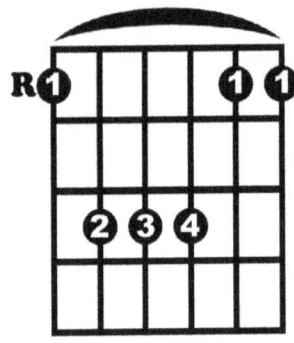 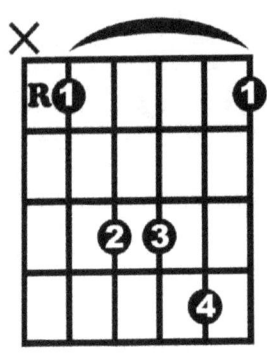 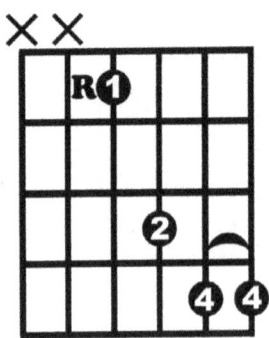

Suspended 2nd (sus2) Chord Shapes

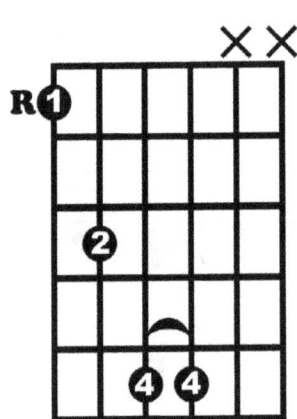 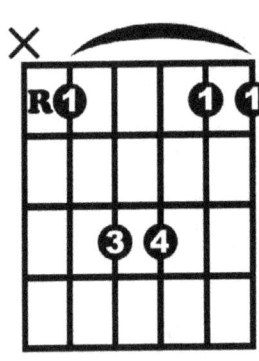 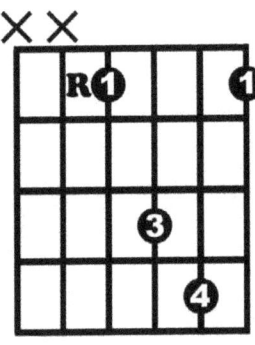

Dominant 7th Suspended 4th (7sus4) Chord Shapes

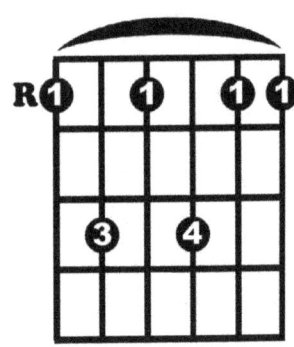 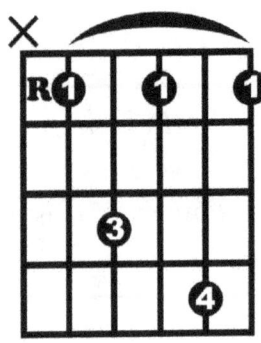 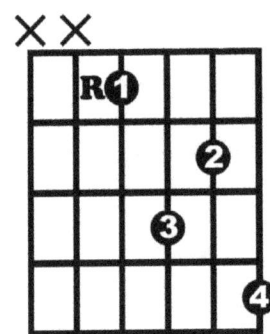

Major 7th (maj7) Chord Shapes

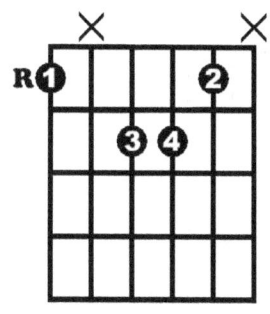 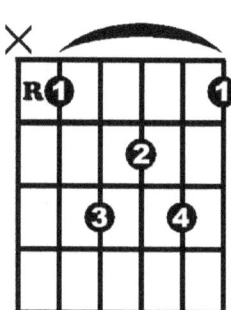 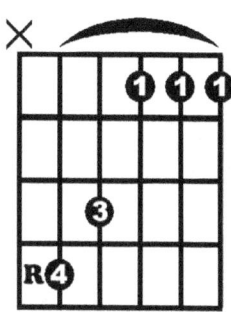 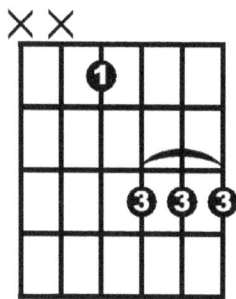

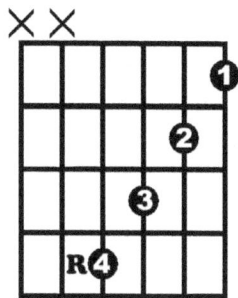

Another commonly used symbol for a major seventh chord is a triangle: Δ

Major 6th (6) Chord Shapes

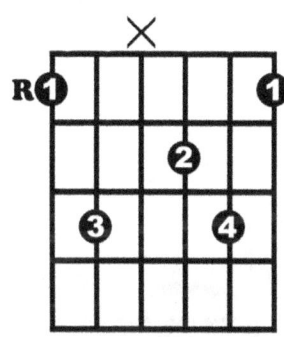 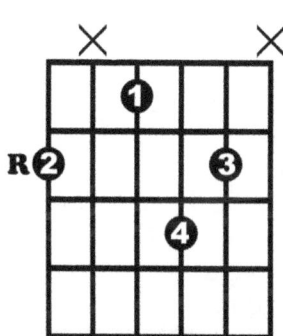 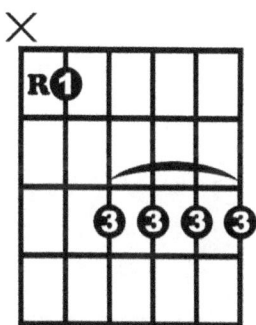 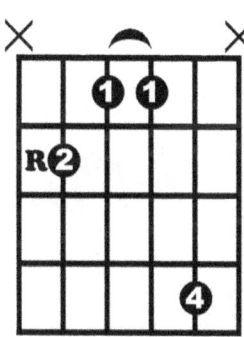

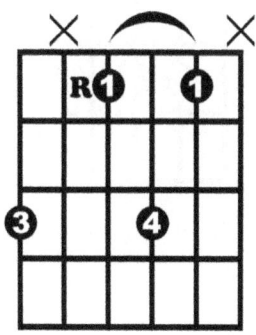

Major 6th chords contain the same notes as minor 7th chords whose roots are a minor 3rd lower. For example, a G major 6th chord contains the same notes as an E minor 7th chord.

Minor 6th (m6) Chord Shapes

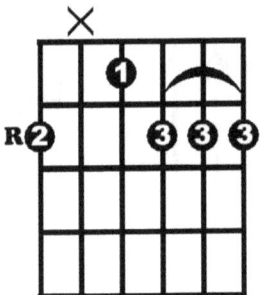 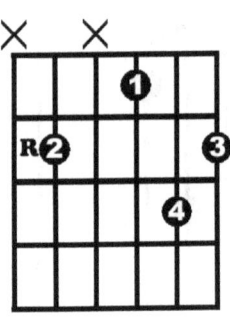 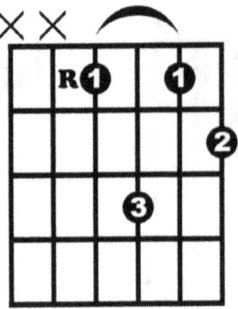

Major 6 - 9 (6/9) Chord Shapes

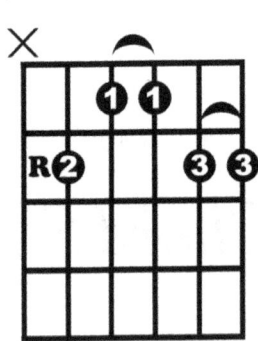 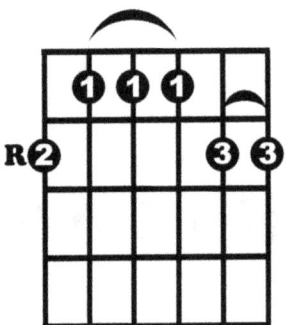

Minor 6 - 9 (m6/9) Chord Shapes

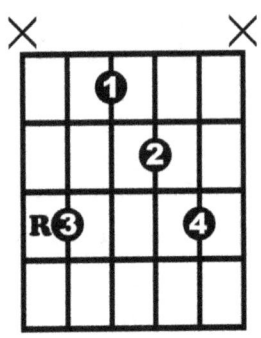 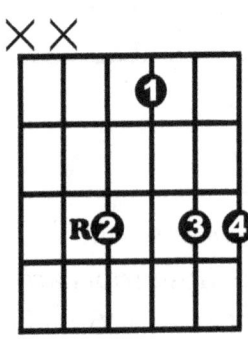 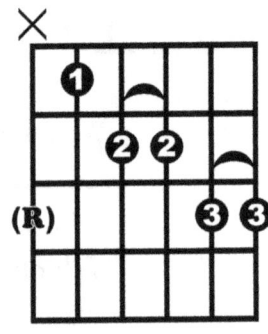 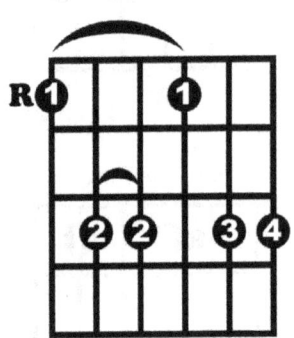

Minor / Major 7th (m(maj7)) Chord Shapes

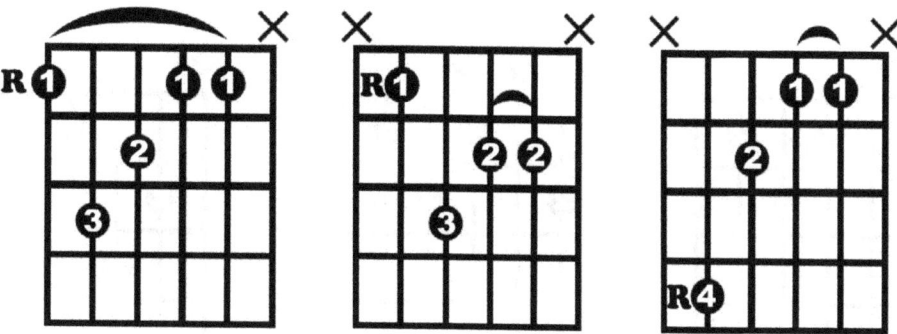

Major Add Nine (add9) Chord Shapes

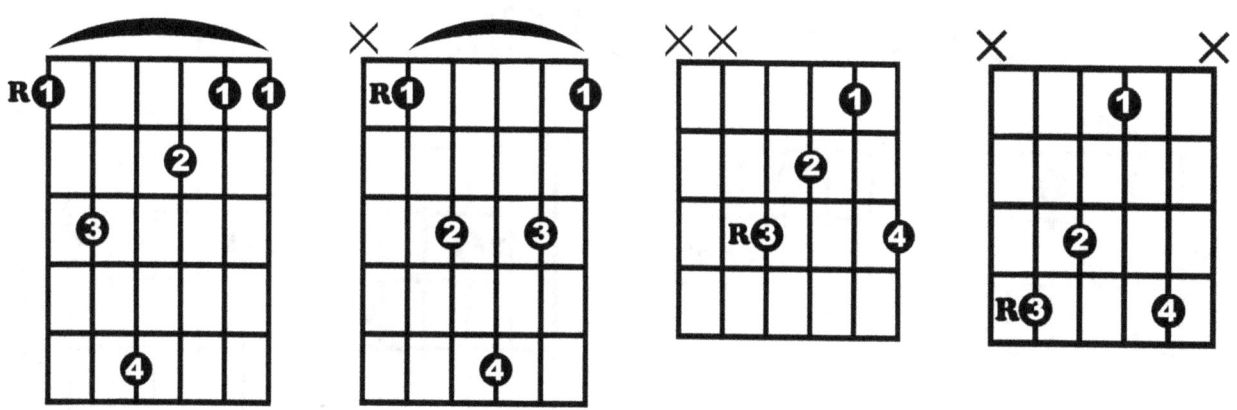

Minor Add Nine (m add9) Chord Shapes

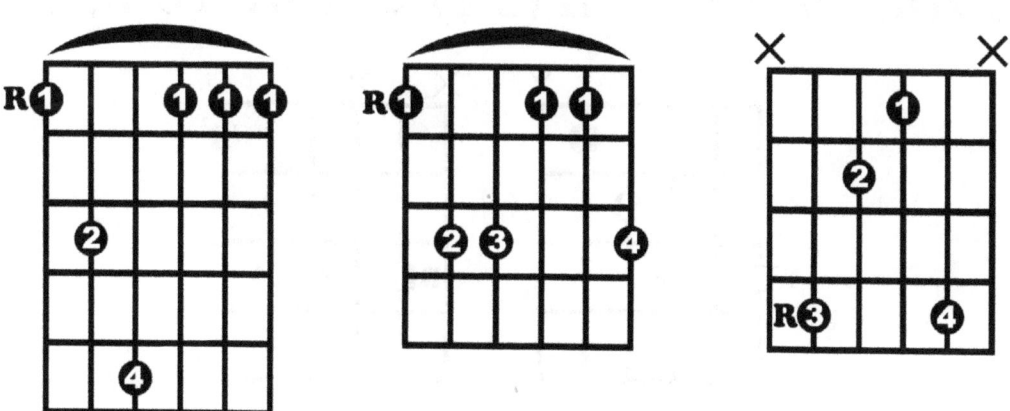

Diminished 7th (dim7 or °7) Chord Shapes

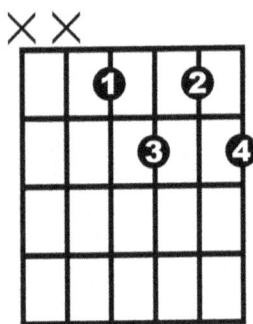 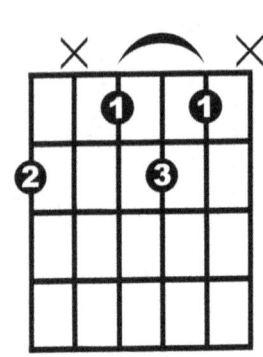 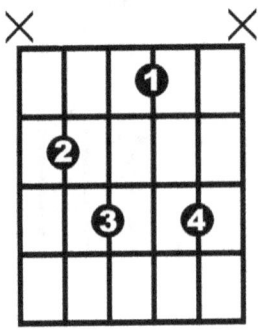

> Any of the notes in a diminished seventh chord can be considered to be the root note. Another symbol for a diminished chord is a small circle: °

Dominant 9th (9) Chord Shapes

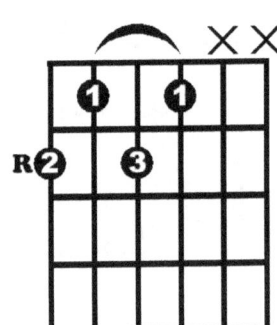 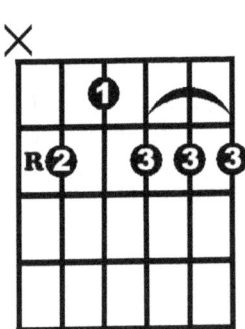 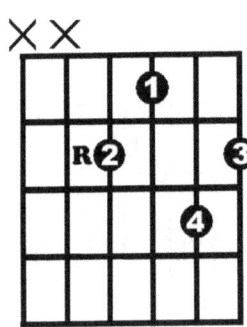 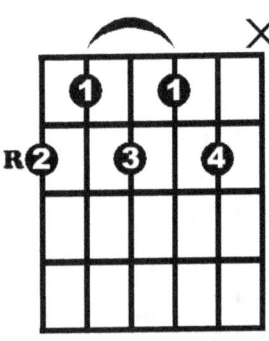

Dominant 11th (11) Chord Shapes

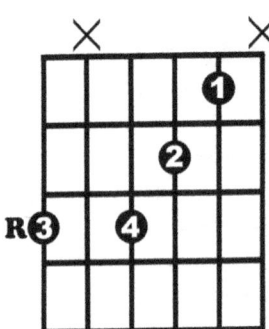 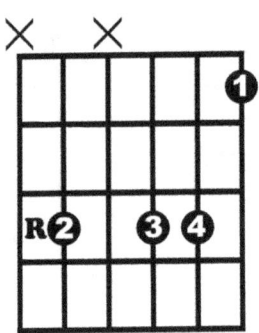

Dominant 13th (13) Chord Shapes

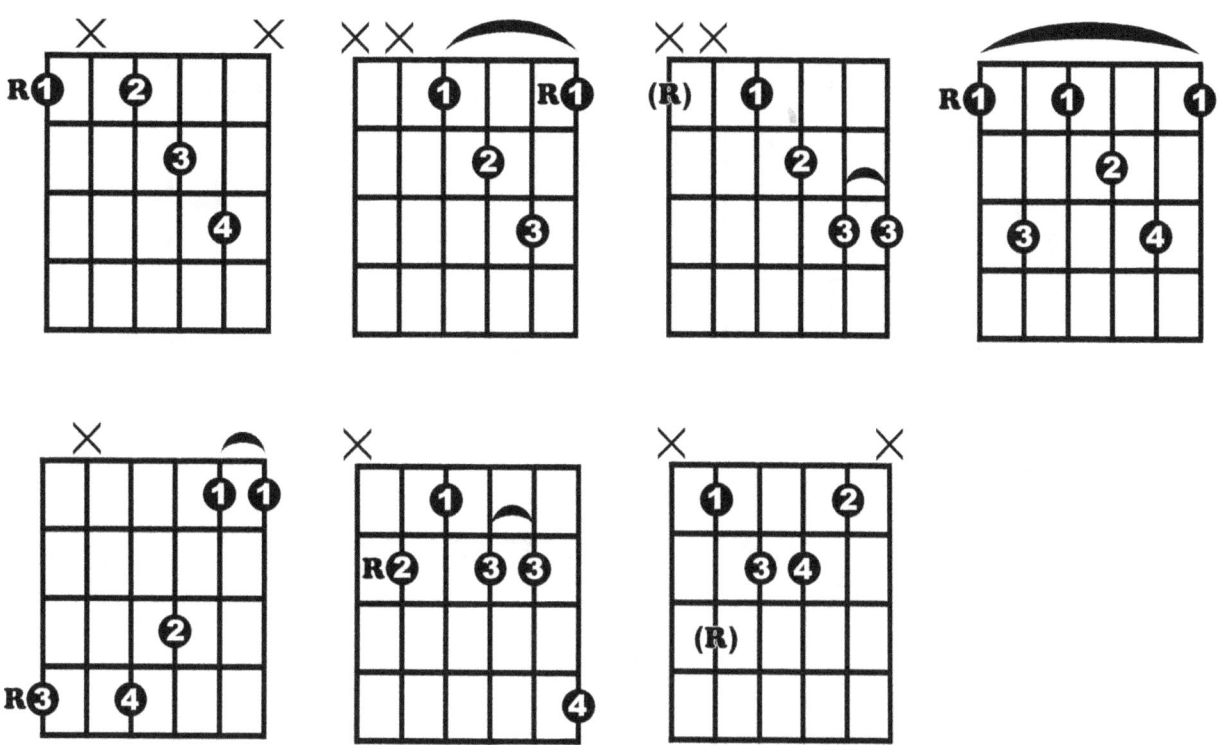

Minor 9th (m9) Chord Shapes

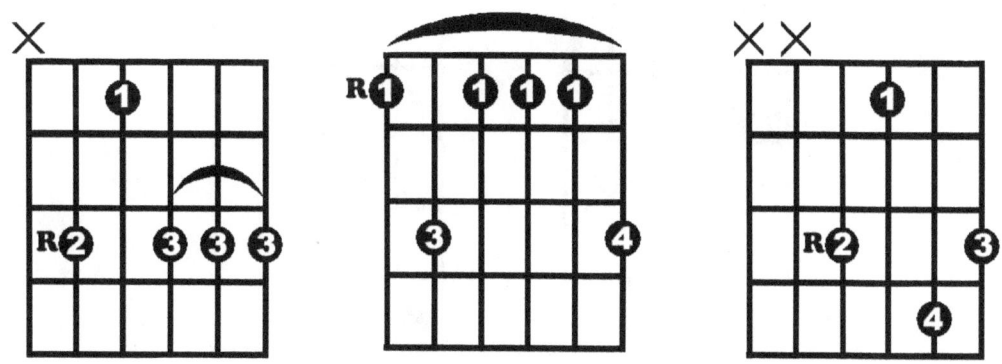

Minor 11th (m11) Chord Shapes

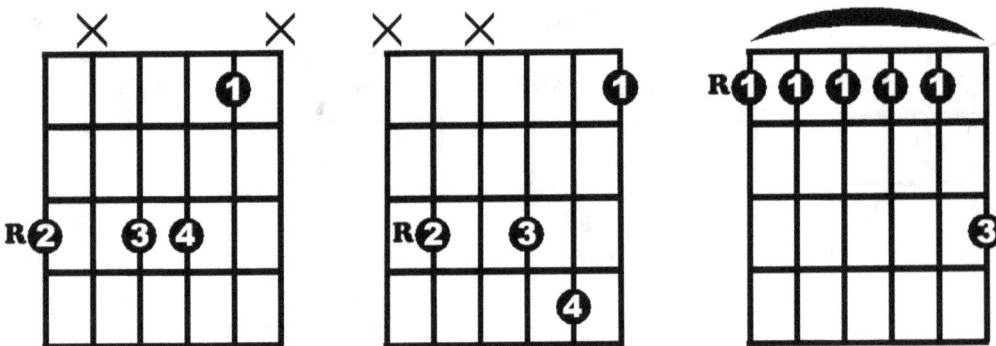

Minor 7th Flat Five (m7♭5) Chord Shapes

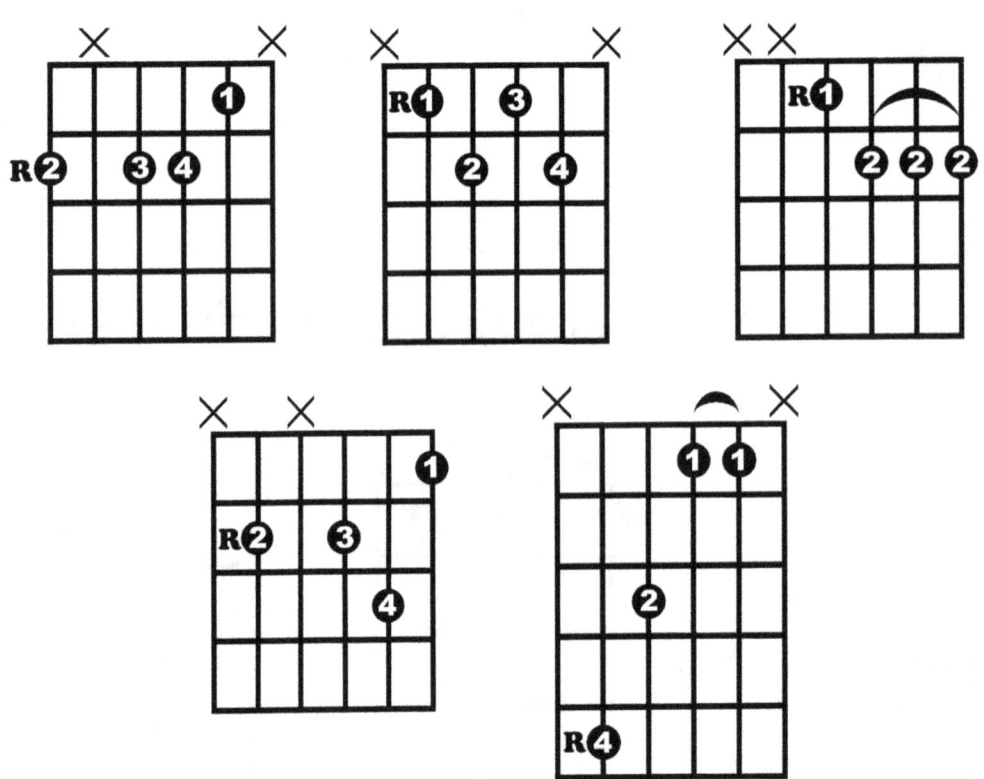

Minor 7th flat five chords are also known as 'half-diminished' chords. A commonly used symbol for a minor 7th flat five chord is a small circle with a dash through it: ⦰

Three-Note Jazz Chords

Jazz guitarists can find themselves having to change chords very quickly in up-tempo numbers. To help them do this, they often play simplified versions of full chords. These three-note chords omit all but the most important notes. Some examples are provided below.

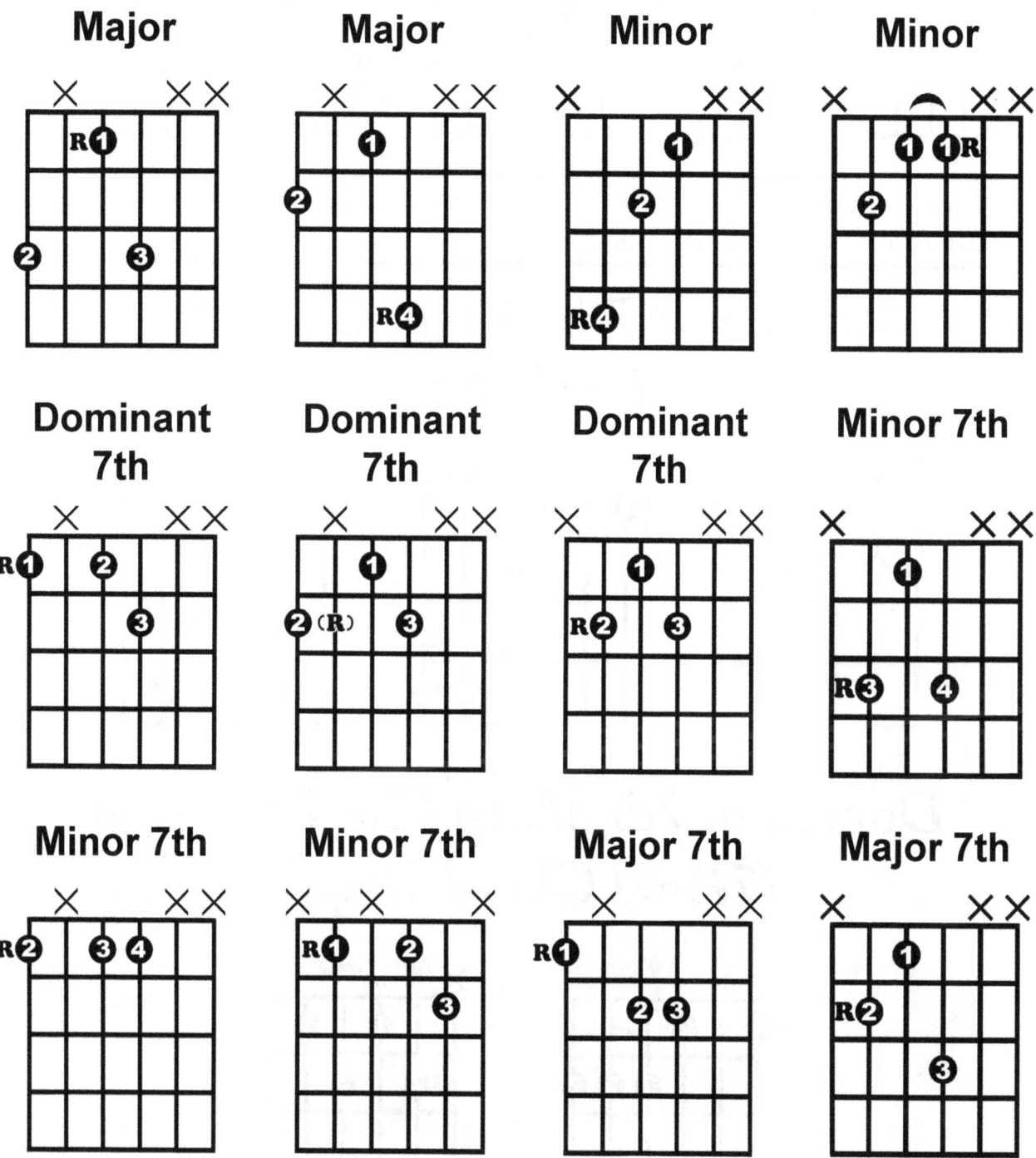

Dominant 7th Augmented (7aug or 7#5) Chord Shapes

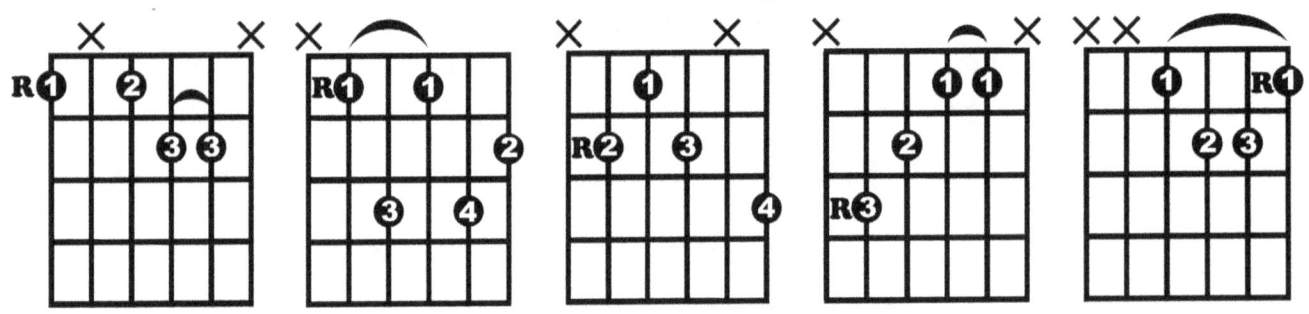

Sharp 5 chords are also called 'augmented' (aug) chords. Another symbol for an augmented chord is a plus (+) sign.

Dominant 7th Sharp Nine (7#9) Chord Shapes

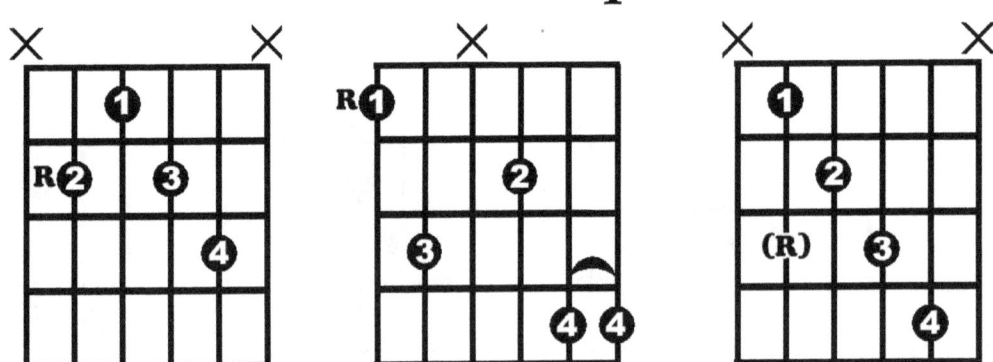

Dominant 7th Sharp Five Flat Nine (7#5b9) Chord Shapes

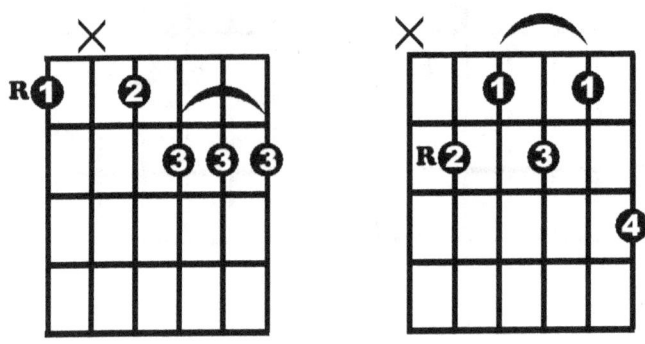

Dominant 7th Sharp Five Sharp Nine (7#5#9) Chord Shapes

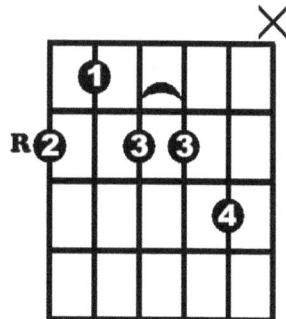 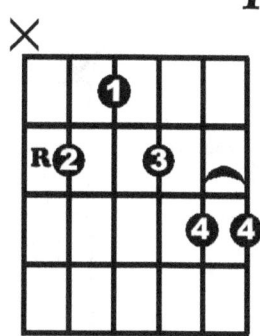 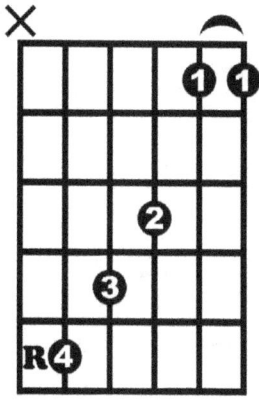

> When played on their own, some of these altered chords can sound quite strange. They are mainly used in jazz, and as you play more of them, you will become accustomed to their sounds. Try playing altered dominant chords instead of standard seventh chords to get used to hearing and playing complex chords.

Dominant 7th Flat Five (7♭5) Chord Shapes

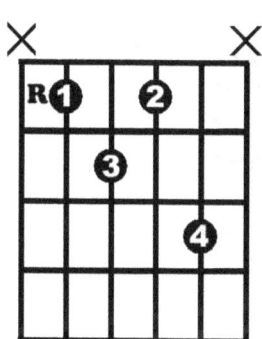 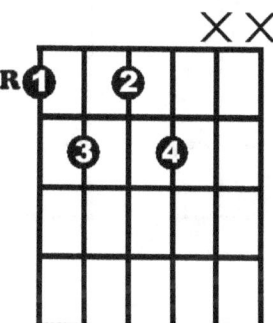

Dominant 7th Flat Nine (7♭9) Chord Shapes

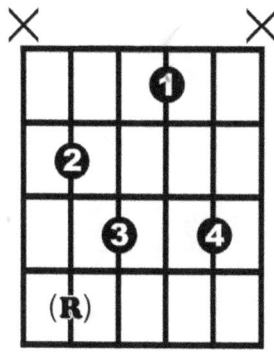 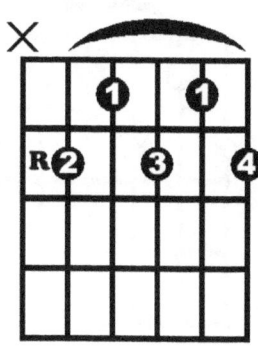 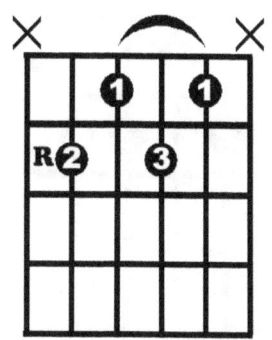 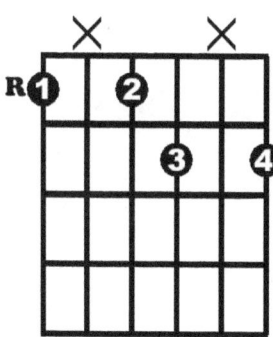

Dominant 7th Flat Five Flat Nine (7♭5♭9) Chord Shapes

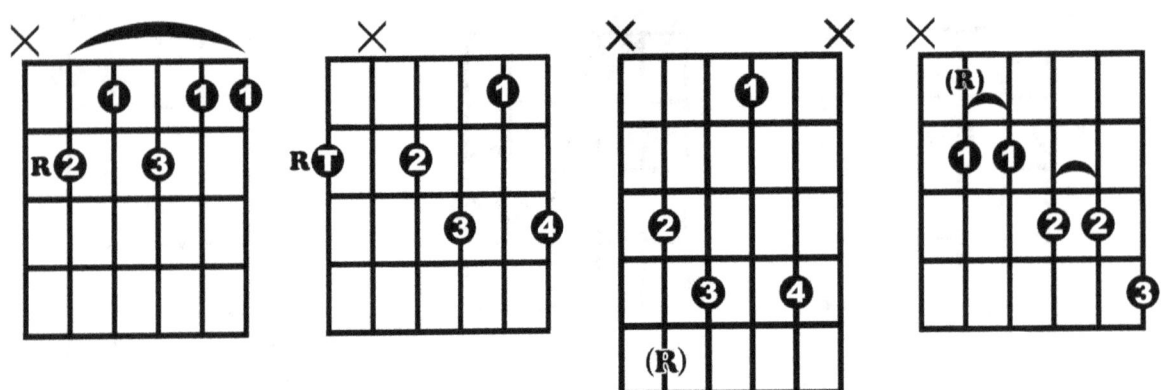

Dominant 9th Sharp Five (9#5) Chord Shapes

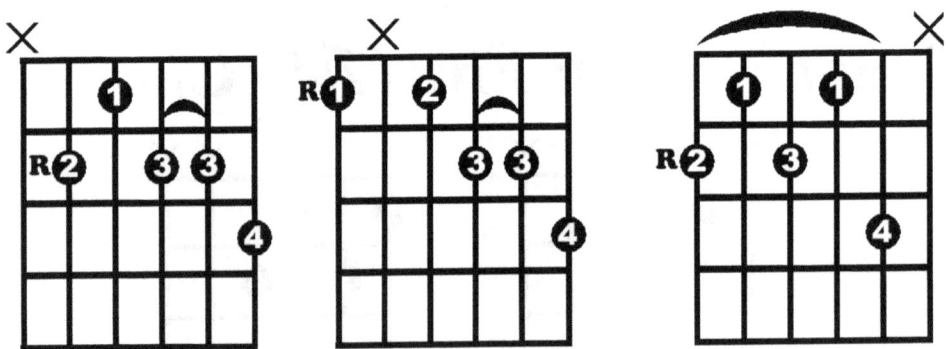

Dominant 9th Flat Five (9♭5) Chord Shapes

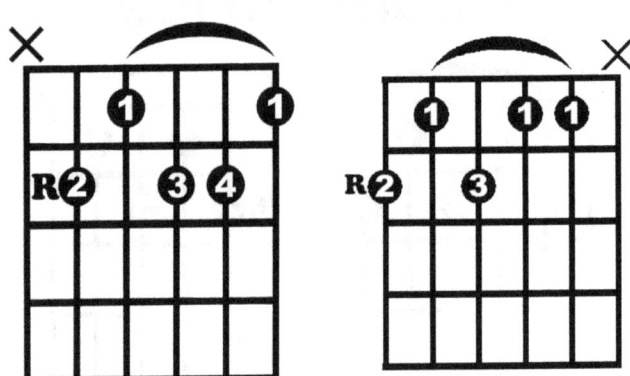

Dominant 13th Flat Five (13♭5) Chord Shapes

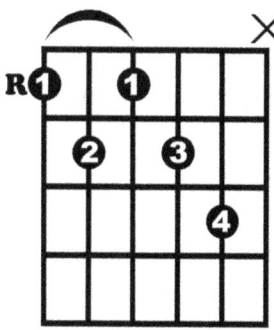 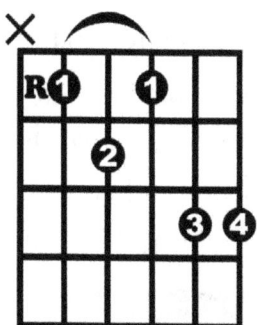

Dominant 13th Flat Nine (13♭9) Chord Shapes

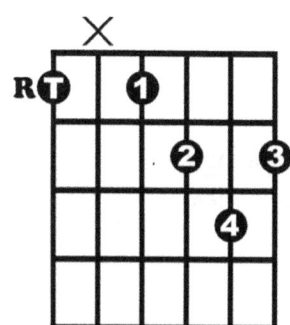 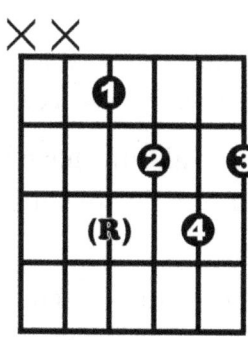 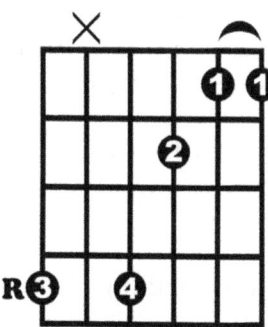 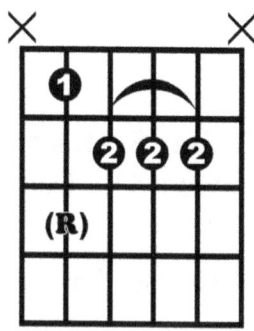

Dominant 13th Sharp Eleven (13#11) Chord Shapes

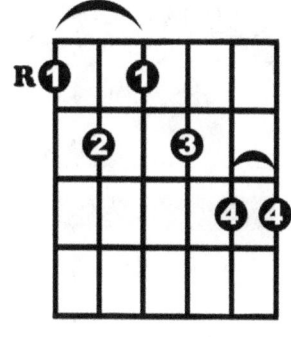 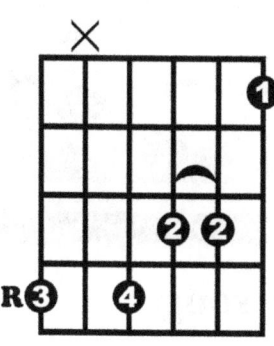 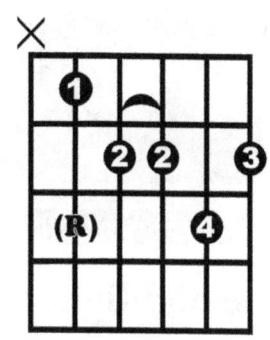 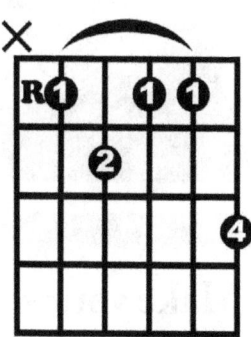

Guitar Command Backing Tracks

Improve Your Lead Guitar Playing With Scales And Modes

You're the lead guitarist.

After the second chorus you have 16 bars to make the song your own.

Is your guitar solo going to be dull, safe and uninspired, or is it going to be a memorable piece of music in its own right?

Break away from the crowd and go with option 2. Use your knowledge of the fretboard to create solos that your fans will love.

Download Guitar Command Backing Tracks from Amazon, iTunes, and many other stores.

Guitar Scales and **Guitar Modes** backing tracks albums have been specially produced for lead guitarists wishing to learn, and practice playing with, scales and modes.

Each track has been written to allow improvisation with a specific scale.

• Learn the scales and modes, then turn them into great music

• Master playing different scales all over the neck and add depth to your solos

Guitar Command Backing Tracks allow you to make the most of your practice time, giving you the advantage you need to stand out from the crowd.

Check out these other awesome backing tracks albums:

Make your solo the highlight of the song.